In the Shadow of History:
A Diplomat's Quest for Truth and Heritage

AF657916

Krishan Chander Dhaka

Qurate
quratebooks.com

In the Shadow of History: A Diplomat's Quest for Truth and Heritage
Krishan Chander Dhaka

Published in 2025

© Published by

Qurate Books Pvt. Ltd.
Goa 403523, India
www.quratebooks.com
Tel: 1800-210-6527, Email: info@quratebooks.com

ISBN: 978-93-58986-35-8

Acknowledgements

I am deeply grateful to my wife, my daughters, my son-in laws and my friends for their unwavering support and encouragement. Their constant nudges, faith and gentle insistence inspired me to transform and transmute my thoughts into the written word and ultimately into this book. Without their love and belief in me, this work would never have come to life.

About the Author

I am a retired officer of Indian Foreign Service (IFS), Ministry of External Affairs, Government of India, New Delhi. A lifelong bibliophile and passionate logophile, I find immense joy in the world of books and words. My personal library - my cherished book corner - is more than just a collection; I consider it the very soul of my home.

-Krishan Chander Dhaka
IFS (Retired)

Foreword

I have had the privilege of knowing Mr. Krishan Chander Dhaka for several years. From the very beginning I recognised his innate flair of writing and often encouraged him to give shape to his thoughts in the form of a book.

This idea, however, materialised only in 2020 when circumstances confined him to his accommodation in London (UK) during the outbreak of COVID-19. The result of that creative confinement is this collection of articles, which I find immensely insightful and marked by engaging honesty, felicity of expression, eloquence and wit. With these qualities, he narrates an unconventional and captivating account of his journey as a diplomat in the Government of India. His thoughtfully written Introduction serves almost as a Précis of the entire book and provides readers with a valuable overview before they delve into the chapters that follow. In successfully navigating the arduous process of getting his book published, Mr. Dhaka has set an inspiring example for all those who aspire to pen their own reflections and experiences.

The publishers - Qurate- Books Pvt. Ltd., under the leadership of Pramod Khera, CEO - deserve our appreciation for their wholehearted cooperation in bringing out this book with such remarkable speed and fine quality of production.

-Colonel (Retired) Mehar Singh Dahiya
Shaurya Chakra.

Contents

Introduction

"In the Shadow of History : A Diplomat's Quest for Truth and Heritage" marks my debut foray into the realm of book writing. The genesis of this idea occurred amidst the unprecedented circumstances of the 2020 Coronavirus pandemic lockdown. In February 2020, my wife and I embarked on a visit to the UK, eagerly anticipating cherished moments with our daughter, son-in-law, and their delightful newborn baby. It was during this time that they fervently encouraged me to capture my reflections and contemplations, derived from a lifetime spent as a diplomat, within the pages of a book. The subsequent lockdown presented a unique occasion for introspection, as it granted me an abundance of time to devote to this endeavor.

Within the pages of my book, I embark on a thought-provoking journey that encompasses a diverse array of subjects, ranging from the ordinary to the profound, all the while straying from the conventional realms of diplomatic discourse. It is important to acknowledge that this book represents my inaugural venture into the realm of writing. Penned solely from the depths of my memory, it bears the imprint of a mind grappling with the limitations imposed by the Corona virus lockdown, which regrettably restricted my access to the vast expanse of knowledge housed within libraries. Despite these constraints, I am resolute in my belief that this book will serve as a vessel for expanding your understanding and, at the very least, offer a fleeting glimpse into the intricacies of my life.

I entered this world in a remote village nestled within the confines of Haryana, an Indian state graced with meager and underdeveloped infrastructure. Reflecting on my early educational journey, I cannot help but find my admission into the village primary school both comical and absurd. It was an era when the notion of education was still a novelty, and the sole educator assigned to our village embarked on a peculiar mission to enroll students for Class 1.

His peculiar admission criteria, now viewed through the lens of hindsight, appeared utterly ludicrous and preposterous. He deemed it necessary for children of the village to have transitioned into the realm of "proper underwear" (an emblem of maturity, it seemed) before they were deemed fit for enrollment. Consequently, a curious spectacle unfolded as parents paraded their children, who had met this rather unconventional requirement, before the teacher to secure a place in the school. The teacher, acting on his own accord, assigned arbitrary dates of birth for each child, tethered to the financial year. This whimsical process yielded a tapestry of amusing birthdates, including my own: the 1st of April, a day synonymous with April Fools' Day.

A year passed, and by what some may deem a quirk of fate or a manifestation of divine grace, circumstances led me to relocate to a neighboring city, where I would reside with my sister and her family. This urban landscape boasted superior amenities and, soon after my arrival, they facilitated my admission into a distinguished school situated in close proximity to their residence.

My academic journey began on a promising note as I excelled in my studies, earning a government scholarship during my time in Class 8 and securing the top position in my school during Class 10. However, fate played a teasing game as I narrowly missed out on the government scholarship by a mere six marks. Upon entering college, I encountered a hurdle as I was urged to pursue the sciences, with the sole aim of becoming a doctor. It is worth noting that during my formative years, the prevailing mindset among Indian parents confined career choices to just two options: medicine or engineering. Naturally, my parents harbored hopes of me pursuing a medical career. Yet, I yearned for a broader horizon beyond the realms of science. Taking the plunge, I listened to the whispers of my soul and transitioned to the humanities, where I could immerse myself in a vast ocean of knowledge.

Devouring books outside the conventional syllabus, I developed a profound interest in linguistics and cultivated a wealth of general knowledge, proving invaluable for competitive examinations. After completing my undergraduate studies at Dayanand College, Hissar, I was granted admission to Panjab University, Chandigarh, where I pursued a Master's degree in English. It was during this time that I participated in numerous competitive examinations. After facing the Union Public Service Commission (UPSC), I was honored to be selected for the esteemed Indian Foreign Service Branch "B" within the Ministry of External Affairs in New Delhi, India.

Over the course of my career, I reached the pinnacle of my profession, ascending to the senior scale of the Indian Foreign Service by the time of my superannuation . Throughout my tenure in the Ministry of External Affairs both my family and I had the privilege of residing in bustling metropolises around the world, including Karachi, Rome, Damascus and Houston. We also visited Beirut, Amman, Ankara, Istanbul, Cape Town, Melbourne, Singapore, Dubai and London. As I share in this book, the life of a diplomat, so to say hilariously ,is often characterized by protocols, alcohol and cholesterol. Looking back, the journey from my humble village of Mochiwali to these vibrant global cities appears surreal, as if a dream had materialized through some divine intervention.

Within the pages of this book, I endeavor to shed light on various diplomatic terms and concepts, drawing from my firsthand experiences and extensive research conducted in libraries. My assignments abroad provided me with diverse perspectives, which, in turn, aided my wife and me in raising three independent and ambitious daughters. Their accomplishments have bestowed upon me the title of a successful father, and I affectionately refer to them as my "three Brontë sisters."

During my assignment in Karachi, Pakistan, an incident caught my attention and ignited a personal quest for understanding my own heritage. While visiting an officer of the Mission for official matters, I found him engrossed in dictating a historical account of the Hun invasions in India. As he concluded his dictation, he asserted that the Huns departed from India due to their inability to withstand the scorching heat, while those who remained, merged with the Indian population, possibly including the Jats.

To my astonishment, as a Jat myself, I failed to identify with the characteristics he attributed to the descendants of the Huns. This revelation prompted me to embark on a journey of self-discovery, delving into extensive research spanning Indian and foreign sources. The culmination of this endeavor is an authentic and untold history of the Jat community, a narrative that holds immense fascination for enthusiasts of history, particularly Jat history.

The Jat community, comprising approximately 80 million individuals, spans across various Indian states such as Punjab, Haryana, Uttar Pradesh, Madhya Pradesh, Rajasthan, Gujarat, and others. Regarded as the sword arm of India, the Jats have historically played a crucial role in defending the motherland and also contribute significantly to the country's agricultural productivity. Notably, the Jats played pivotal roles in securing victory for the British in both of the great wars.

Within the pages of this book, I endeavor to present an authentic account of Jat history, shedding light on their unique identity, achievements, and contributions to India. It is my hope that this exploration into the untold past of the Jat community will captivate the hearts and minds of those intrigued by the rich tapestry of history.

My life's journey has intertwined with significant historical events, leaving an indelible mark on my experiences. From the India-China War of 1962 to the India-Pakistan Wars of 1965 and 1971, these pivotal moments have shaped my perspectives and driven me to conduct extensive research. Within the pages of this book, I offer my insights and reflections on these wars, shedding light on lesser-known aspects and highlighting the contributions of remarkable historical figures who have often been overlooked or not given their due recognition.

I delve into the lives and achievements of extraordinary individuals such as the illustrious King Mahendra Pratap of Mursan, the visionary Deenbandhu Sir Chhotu Ram, the indomitable Netaji Subhas Chandra Bose, and the legendary Maharaja Surajmal. These figures, among others, have left an indelible impact on history, and it is my endeavor to bring their stories to the forefront.

Furthermore, I recount my personal experiences during my assignments in Karachi, Rome, Damascus, and Houston. These vibrant cities have provided a backdrop for unique encounters, cultural exchanges, and insights into the global dynamics that have shaped our world. By sharing these anecdotes and reflections, I aim to offer readers a glimpse into the diverse tapestry of my diplomatic stints in different corners of the world.

Through this book, I hope to illuminate hidden facets of history, shed light on forgotten heroes, and provide a personal account of my own remarkable journey. It is my aspiration that readers will find inspiration and a deeper understanding of the events and individuals that have played significant roles in shaping our shared history.

In my exploration of life's myriad facets, I have delved into the realm of spirituality. One particular work that has captivated my attention is the book "Death & After" authored by the late Justice VR Krishna Iyer, a distinguished former Judge of the Indian Supreme Court. Within the pages of this thought-provoking book, Justice Iyer propounds the belief that upon our demise, our soul transcends its earthly vessel.

I found this book to be truly intriguing, as it delves into profound questions surrounding life, death, and the nature of our existence beyond the physical realm. Justice Iyer's perspective offers a fresh perspective and prompts contemplation on the mysteries that lie beyond our mortal boundaries.

Through my own reflections and insights garnered from Justice Iyer's work, I have endeavored to shed light on this captivating subject within the pages of my own writing. It is my hope that readers will find themselves equally captivated by the profound concepts and intriguing ideas put forth in "Death & After," as we delve into the enigmatic realm of spirituality and contemplate the mysteries that await us beyond the confines of our earthly existence.

Within the pages of my book, I delve into the complex and tumultuous history of Jammu and Kashmir. I offer my perspectives on the Partition of India in 1947, expressing my belief in its futility due to the lack of tangible benefits it provided to both Hindus and Muslims on the subcontinent. Instead, this Partition unleashed one of the most devastating catastrophes in human memory. Countless lives were lost, and countless more were displaced as a result.

It is worth noting that prior to the Partition , Hinduism and Islam had coexisted on the soil of India for centuries without significant conflict. The Partition marked an aberration in this history, where religious lines were drawn to separate India and Pakistan, leading to unprecedented violence and upheaval.

In addition to historical analysis, I offer reviews of articles published in newspapers, providing my own insights and critical examination. The farmers' agitation, a significant contemporary issue, has also received my attention, as I explore and express my views on this important movement.

Furthermore, I have dedicated sections of my book to reviewing the NCERT history books prescribed in Indian schools, aiming to provide an informed perspective on their content and accuracy.

Among the pages, you will also find reflections on esteemed personalities such as Dr. Ram Dhan Singh, Kisan Kesari Baldev Ram Mirdha, Chaudhary Devi Lal, Dr. Balram Jakhar, and Dr. Sarup Singh. These individuals have left a lasting impact on their respective fields and have contributed significantly to the social fabric of our nation.

Through these diverse topics and discussions, I hope to provide readers with a comprehensive and thought-provoking exploration of history, contemporary issues, and remarkable personalities. It is my aspiration that these insights will contribute to a greater understanding of our past, present, and the world we inhabit.

I sincerely hope that my chronicles will provide you with an enjoyable and thought-provoking reading experience, just as writing them has brought me immense joy and fulfillment. It is my aspiration that the words penned within these pages will spark curiosity, ignite introspection, and leave a lasting impression on your mind.

Writing this book has been a labor of love, driven by a desire to share my perspectives, insights, and experiences with readers like you. I have poured my heart and soul into crafting these musings, with the hope that they will resonate with you on a personal level and perhaps even inspire new thoughts and ideas.

Thank you for embarking on this literary journey with me. It is my utmost pleasure to have the opportunity to share my thoughts and reflections with you, and I am grateful for your readership. May this book offer you a world of contemplation, discovery, and enjoyment as we traverse the realms of history, spirituality, personal experiences, and much more together. Happy reading!

Krishan Chander Dhaka
IFS (Retired) from
the Ministry of External Affairs,
New Delhi
Government of India

1

My Early Life

I was born in the small, sleepy and non-descript village of Mochiwali in Sirsa district, Haryana, India. The memories of my childhood flood my mind vividly. Our village was situated in a semi-desert with sprawling sand dunes and lacked paved roads. Camels and horses were the primary modes of travel, and my father's prized possessions included a camel and a horse.

Fortunately, our village was blessed with a significant canal that provided irrigation to our agricultural fields. This canal had historical significance, as it was originally dug by the Muslim King Firuz Shah Tughlak (1351-1388 AD) but had become buried over time. During a famine in 1899-1900 AD, the British constructed a new canal in the same location to provide employment to the affected farmers.

Nowadays, the landscape has transformed dramatically. Tractors and tube wells have revolutionized farming, making it more efficient and scientifically driven. The lives of farmers have been greatly eased by these advancements.

The transition from the rustic ways of my childhood to the modern practices of today has been remarkable, shaping my understanding of progress and the evolution of agriculture. Allow me to share a childhood incident that remains etched in my memory. During the winter season, my mother made delicious "pinni" (a sweet treat made from wheat flour, ghee, sugar, and dry fruits). Excitedly, I anticipated enjoying this special treat. However, my brother, who was senior to me, informed me that the "pinni" was exclusively reserved for our two eldest brothers, who worked strenuously on the agricultural farm. He suggested we protest by refusing to wake up early for morning tea and by abstaining from meals. Despite my anger, I expressed my inability to remain without food.

Moved by my predicament, my brother promised to secretly bring me food. As we whispered our rebellious plans in bed, our eldest brother, who happened to overhear and eavesdrop us, promptly informed our mother about our secret rebellion. We felt embarrassed when our mother approached us. However, she assured us that she would prepare "pinni" for us later in the day, and our rebellion swiftly fizzled out.

At that tender age of around three years, I was reminded of the limits of my protest and learned the importance of obedience and understanding. This incident serves as a poignant reminder of the innocence and lessons learned during my early childhood.

My father, despite lacking formal education, was raised with great care by his paternal uncle ("tau") Ch. Hari Chand, after the untimely demise of my grandparents when my father was just eighteen months old. However, during the First World War, a mandate from the British rulers required one person from each family to join the British Indian army. In response, my father's "tau" Ch. Hari Chand made the decision to enlist and serve in the Camel Squad, experiencing the rigors of battle in the Middle East. Remarkably, he returned home alive but succumbed to the hardships he faced during the war a few years later.

During my tenure at the Ministry of External Affairs, I resided near India Gate, an iconic monument designed by Sir Edwin Lutyens and completed in 1931. One day, while visiting India Gate, I discovered that the names of soldiers who had lost their lives in the Afghan Wars and the First World War were engraved on its stones. Following the India-Pakistan War of 1971, the Government of India established the "Amar Jawan Jyoti" Memorial near India Gate to honor Indian soldiers who made the ultimate sacrifice for their country. Additionally, a National War Memorial was inaugurated on February 25, 2019, near the canopy of India Gate by the Prime Minister of India, serving as a tribute to the nation's fallen heroes.

These experiences and encounters with historical memorials have deepened my appreciation for the sacrifices made by brave soldiers and their enduring legacy.

Fortunately, my village was blessed with a railway station just two kilometers away. At the tender age of five, I experienced the joy of my first train journey. The train brought a touch of modernity to our humble village, enhancing its overall ambiance.

Along National Highway No. 10, there was an impromptu bus stop situated approximately five kilometers from my village. However, bus drivers often chose to halt their vehicles either before or after the designated stop arbitrarily.This practice made it challenging for passengers, as only those who were physically fit could manage to board the bus. On one occasion, my mother decided to visit her parental home with my eldest brother, carrying my youngest brother in her arms. Regrettably, the bus driver stopped the bus prior to the designated location where passengers were waiting. Despite the passengers' sprint to catch the bus, my mother was unable to board and had to return home. Undeterred, she resolved to make a more determined attempt the following day. Instead, she shared the sweets she had prepared for her parents' family with us, spreading a sense of consolation amidst our disappointment.

These simple yet memorable experiences highlight the nuances of transportation in rural areas and the determination of individuals like my mother to overcome obstacles in their journeys.

Instances like these were not isolated incidents but rather a common practice that highlighted the lack of empathy among individuals. As I grew older, I would often travel alone and rightfully purchase a half-ticket based on my age when boarding trains. However, there was a particular ticket clerk who displayed a devious nature. Despite requesting a half-ticket, he would insist that I was eligible for a full ticket, only to charge me for a full ticket and provide me with a half-ticket instead. His cunning tactics were an unscrupulous way to extort money.

Furthermore, an unfortunate incident occurred involving my father, who held a prominent position in our village and had been elected as a member of the village Panchayat. One day, while my father was tending to his agricultural fields, a murder took place in our village, prompting the police to seek out the Sarpanch and other Panchayat members. Astonishingly, the police arrived at our agriculture farm and treated my father with disrespect and misconduct. This incident led my father to vow never to participate in any Panchayat elections again. It is disheartening to acknowledge that the Indian police force continues to bear the remnants of its colonial past.

These experiences shed light on the challenges faced by individuals within society and the need for empathy, integrity, and a fair justice system to ensure a harmonious environment for all.

During my time in the 8th standard, I observed that the freedom of the press allowed for mischievous reporting. Regrettably, a murder occurred in my village, and the Tribune English newspaper published an article stating, "A Jat boy named Kishna, aged 20 years, allegedly shot and killed two individuals in Mochiwali village, Sirsa district. One of the victims was a village shopkeeper who had denied him further credit, and the other was the accused's uncle, with whom he had a land dispute." To this day, I question the necessity of mentioning the delinquent's caste in the report.

•••

2

Education and Selection in Indian Foreign Service

Comparing our past with the present, it's clear how primitive our circumstances once were. In my village, electricity was nonexistent, and the entire community shared just two transistors. Our education system was laughable; a tiny primary school, only reaching the 5th standard, sat a kilometer away. Enrollment was a comical affair. I recall one day when a teacher visited, announcing that only children wearing underwear would be accepted. Standing nearby, I was singled out for inspection. After a brief assessment, the teacher, aided by a village elder, determined I was seven years old and assigned a birthdate. Little did I realize then, the significance this arbitrary date would later hold. When I pursued employment, this fabricated birthdate sabotaged my eligibility by falsely aging me two years.

One fateful day, the teacher ordered all four of the fifth graders to round up students enrolled in the first standard. I found myself ambushed by two classmates, each gripping my hands and legs as they forcibly dragged me to school, a kilometer's distance away. The teacher's furious banging of his stick echoed, a menacing backdrop to my reluctant journey. Like a defeated soldier, I entered the school premises under duress.

Upon returning home after school, I recounted the harrowing experience to my parents. Instead of sympathizing with my plight, they urged me to attend school willingly. To aid my education, they provided funds to purchase essential supplies like a primer, counting table, and slate.

A turning point came when my sister and brother-in-law, who resided in Sonepat city where my brother-in-law had secured a government job, invited me to stay with them for a few months. Initially intended to help their son adjust to city life, I unexpectedly found myself immersed in a world of opportunity. My family held lofty aspirations for my future, believing that access to education in the city could pave the way for success. With their support, I acquired the necessary materials for learning, including a primer and other essential tools.

After my temporary return to the village, I faced envy from fellow students due to my knowledge and well-groomed appearance. However, my family's relocation to Bhatgaon, a village near Sonipat, marked a new chapter in my education. Enrolled in the second standard, I encountered a daily challenge from a boy my size who sought to test my wrestling prowess. Accepting his challenge one day, I emerged victorious under the watchful eye of our teacher, establishing my dominance both academically and physically. Recognizing my leadership potential, I was appointed as the class monitor, a role I embraced wholeheartedly.

From there, I maintained my academic excellence, consistently securing the top position in each class. My dedication was rewarded with a government scholarship in the eighth grade. Although I narrowly missed out on another scholarship in the tenth grade, my achievements propelled me towards the next milestone: college.

However, my initial foray into college was tumultuous. I was steered towards a career in medicine without my aptitude, I found myself struggling. The confines of a science stream with a focus on Biology felt restrictive, akin to swimming in a pond whereas I longed to explore the vastness of the ocean in pursuit of knowledge.

One day, following the call of my soul, I made a pivotal decision to switch to the Humanities stream. Moving into the college hostel, I delved into a vast array of general books beyond the confines of the syllabus. Immersing myself in literature, I honed my command of the English language and expanded my reservoir of general knowledge.

Upon graduating, I pursued a Master's degree in English at Panjab University in Chandigarh. It was during this time that I resolved to embark on a path of competitive examinations. Through dedication and determination, I secured a position in Branch "B" of the Indian Foreign Service through UPSC.

Over the years, I climbed the ranks within the service, eventually reaching the zenith of my career in the senior scale of the IFS within the Ministry of External Affairs, Government of India, by the time of my superannuation.

After securing a position in the government, I entered into matrimony. There was only one proposal, where the bride was a graduate. Without hesitation, we accepted the proposal, even though I hadn't laid eyes on my future wife prior to our marriage.

Subsequently, as I embarked on postings abroad, my wife became an indispensable source of support and strength. Possessing exceptional sartorial and culinary skills, she exudes sophistication and culture.In fact, she is an aesthete .She is extraordinarily gifted in that she knows Abacus mathematics and Vedic mathematics. She taught students in these two disciplines. Over the years, she has cultivated a diverse repertoire, demonstrating her versatility and adaptability.

It wouldn't be an exaggeration to say that she is the proverbial wind beneath my wings, propelling me forward and uplifting me in every endeavor.

My wife's family boasts significant connections in Haryana's political landscape. Her maternal grandfather, Chaudhary Ganpat Singh Sihag, hailed from Chautala village and was the first cousin of the formidable Haryana leader, Chaudhary Devi Lal. It is etched in history that Chaudhary Devi Lal ascended to the position of Chief Minister of Haryana in 1978 and subsequently in 1987 also.

Adding to this lineage, my wife's maternal uncle, Dr. K. V. Singh, served as Officer on Special Duty (OSD) to Chaudhary Devi Lal. Chaudhary Devi Lal's political influence extended beyond Haryana; he made significant strides in national politics during the General Elections of 1989. The air was filled with slogans proclaiming that "Tau (Chaudhary Devi Lal) poora tolega or Lal Qile se bolega," signifying his anticipated elevation to Prime Minister and the expectation that he would address the nation from the Red Fort.

Indeed, on December 1st, 1989, Chaudhary Devi Lal was unanimously chosen as the Prime Minister of India. However, he made the unexpected decision to pass this honor to Shri V. P. Singh, a move that perplexed historians and remains shrouded in mystery. Opting instead to serve as Deputy Prime Minister, Chaudhary Devi Lal earned the endearing title of "Tau" of the nation.

Through my wife's familial ties with the Chaudhary Devi Lal family, I found myself inadvertently connected with the influential figures and elite circles of Jats in Haryana, Punjab, and Rajasthan.

Throughout my career in the Indian Foreign Service, I was privileged to be posted to various countries, each presenting unique challenges and opportunities. Reflecting on my humble beginnings in a rural village devoid of prospects, the trajectory of my life seemed nothing short of miraculous. The transition from the mofussil village to foreign metropolises felt like a manifestation of divine intervention, fulfilling a dream I had scarcely dared to entertain.

These assignments abroad not only broadened my professional horizons but also nurtured a cosmopolitan perspective within me. However, my greatest source of pride and fulfillment lies in the achievements of my three daughters. Through their intelligence and hard work, they have attained esteemed positions outside of India, serving as a testament to their determination and resilience.

In February 2020, I traveled to London to be with my daughter, son-in-law, and their newborn son. However, the unforeseen onset of the pandemic and subsequent closure of airspace prevented my return to India. It was during this period of unexpected confinement that my daughter and son-in-law encouraged me to channel my thoughts into writing for the benefit of the general public. Thus, began my new adventure, where I embarked on sharing my reflections and musings with the world.

●●●

3

A Hilarious Anecdote

Once upon a time, during my posting at the Indian Embassy in Rome, I worked in the Visa and Passport Division. Two local employees, shrewd and intelligent brothers, decided they wanted to take a month off together to visit India. They became extra courteous to me, greeting me with cheerful "good mornings" and "good evenings," which, of course, impressed me.

One day, they approached me with their request, and I agreed, saying I didn't mind doing a bit of extra work while Miss Marina would cover for them. When I conveyed this to the administration, one officer insisted I formally consent to their leave. I replied in my classic Haryanavi style, "If Rama and Lakshmana wanted to go together, how could I object?" It's a common trait in Haryanavi culture to jump into decisions before thinking them through!

The next day, as phone calls flooded in, I realized I was in trouble—I didn't know Italian! Miss Marina handled a few calls but soon admitted she couldn't manage them all. So, I decided to learn Italian, thinking of how my daughter picked it up unwittingly and effortlessly by watching cartoons.

After work, I set off on foot to catch the bus home, trying to figure out how to solve this linguistic crisis. I preferred taking the bus to avoid the hassle of parking. When I reached home, my wife noticed my glum demeanor, but I put on a brave face, had dinner early, and went to bed to mull over the problem.

In the middle of the night, it struck me: my local employee John often said "visto turistico," which meant "tourist visa." I thought, "Maybe that's my ticket!"

The next day, I arrived at the office brimming with optimism. I took notes from Miss Marina on the visa procedure, translating it into a mix of Hindi and Italian: "Visto turistico per lei India validita terre mesi sono necessari e seventi documenti modulo completo terre photo formato te serra orario nove do desi pagare wentun mila se cento lire."

I started reciting this to every caller, and to my surprise, out of ten callers, nine responded with "wa benne," which I took as a sign of approval! Somehow, I had turned the chaos into a workable solution.

One day, our Ambassador walked in while I was enthusiastically chatting away in "Italian." He patted me on the back, praising my newfound fluency. However, some callers later told the receptionist that I was speaking Italian well but wasn't answering their actual questions. It turned out their inquiries were quite different from the visa procedure!

Our receptionist didn't mind answering a couple of calls, but he certainly didn't want to field them all. This incident taught me a valuable lesson: to be cautious and think things through before leaping into action. Ultimately, I managed to tackle the situation in a hilariously improvisational way, embodying the quintessential Indian spirit of "jugaad," a term famously lauded by Sir Mark Tully, former Bureau Chief of BBC in New Delhi.

●●●

4

First Brush with Bureaucracy

In 1974, my younger brother received a national scholarship in 10th grade for his academic excellence and transitioned to college. The college required us to obtain an income certificate, so we filled out the necessary form and secured our annual income details from the local Patwari.

I headed to the Tehsil office, but upon arrival, we learned that the Tehsildar was on leave, and the Naib Tehsildar was handling his duties. We approached him, finding him seated on a pedestal in a grand, old colonial building, flanked by two witness boxes. Despite our polite request for his signature and stamp, he brusquely dismissed us.

My elder brother made a heartfelt plea, but the Naib Tehsildar insisted we provide exhaustive details about our father's agricultural land—something that was entirely unnecessary for our purpose. I tried to interject, but he barked at me, questioning my age as if it determined my right to speak to a government official. He embodied the arrogance of authority, behaving as if he were a demigod.

Just then, a gun-wielding policeman appeared, menacingly shooing us away. Frustrated, we decided to escalate the matter to the Sub Divisional Magistrate (SDM). My brother reached out to a government doctor who had connections with the SDM. After some time, the doctor emerged from the SDM's office with the required signature and seal, and we breathed a sigh of relief.

However, our ordeal didn't end there. We submitted the signed document to the college administration, which forwarded it to Chandigarh, the state government headquarters. A year passed with no news about the scholarship. We even sent a letter to the concerned office in Chandigarh, only to have it returned in another envelope.

In the midst of the Emergency period in India, we decided to take a bold step. We sent a registered letter to the Chief Minister of Haryana. Miraculously, two weeks later, our college received a fat cheque covering the entire year's scholarship amount. It was more than enough to manage our college and hostel expenses for three months, so we didn't have to return home for money during that time.

Reflecting on this experience, I still wonder why bureaucracy often complicates life for the common man. It's disheartening to think that, even after 70 years of independence, we continue to navigate a bureaucratic maze.

(As a side note, my younger brother eventually rose to become the MD of a leading Milk plant in Jaipur, Rajasthan.)

●●●

5

Demystifying Diplomatic Terms : Insights from My Tenure at the Ministry of External Affairs

Throughout my tenure at the Ministry of External Affairs, I conducted research yielding valuable information pertinent to general knowledge.

Here I am trying to demystify some commonly misunderstood diplomatic terms.

(a) Why is the Ministry of External Affairs in India not called the Ministry of Foreign Affairs? The Ministry of External Affairs in India is not referred to as the Ministry of Foreign Affairs due to historical reasons. When India gained independence on August 15, 1947, it inherited a complex geopolitical landscape with over 500 princely states. While most of these states acceded to either India or Pakistan, issues persisted with states like Hyderabad, Junagadh, and Jammu & Kashmir, which drew international attention, including involvement from the United Nations.

To reflect its expanded role in managing both external affairs and the complexities of its internal states on the international stage, the Indian government chose to name its foreign ministry the Ministry of External Affairs. This nomenclature underscores its responsibility not only for traditional external affairs but also for representing the interests of states like Hyderabad, Junagadh, and Jammu & Kashmir in international forums such as the United Nations.

(b) Who is a Gazetted Officer? The Bengal Gazette holds the distinction of being India's inaugural newspaper. Originating during the British colonial era, it introduced the practice of printing the names of certain officers and their career activities, thus creating the concept of Gazetted Officers. These individuals were highly esteemed within their respective fields. Notably, the police were required to obtain permission from their departments before arresting Gazetted Officers for any misconduct.

Furthermore, Gazetted Officers were entrusted with the authority to authenticate certain documents. In contemporary times, the career activities of specific officers, including Gazetted Officers, are often published in newspapers, a practice commonly referred to as Gazette Notification.

(c) What is a passport? A passport serves as a crucial travel document for individuals seeking to travel abroad, typically accompanied by a visa. In India, there are three primary types of passports:

1. Ordinary Passport: Issued to regular citizens of the country for international travel purposes.
2. Diplomatic Passport: Reserved for diplomats, ministers, members of parliament (MPs), members of legislative assemblies (MLAs), chief ministers, or individuals authorized by the government for specific roles.
3. Official Passport: Granted to officials of the Ministry of External Affairs who are non-diplomats, as well as designated officers of other ministries and departments.

In addition to these passports, there is also provision for an Emergency Certificate. This one-way travel document is issued to nationals of the country who have lost their passport while abroad and need to return to India immediately. It facilitates their travel back to India under urgent circumstances.

(d) What is a Visa? A visa is an official authorization or permission granted by the foreign mission of a country, allowing an individual to enter and stay within that country for a specified period. In certain cases, travelers with connecting flights may be permitted to stay within the confines of an airport for up to 72 hours without requiring a visa. However, if they wish to exit the airport during this layover period, they must obtain a prior Transit Visa. This visa facilitates temporary entry into the country for the purpose of transitioning to their final destination.

(e) What is a Note Verbale? A Note Verbale is a formal written communication exchanged between the Foreign Ministry of a country and the Foreign Missions accredited within that country, or vice versa. Typically, this form of communication is used when the Head of Mission of a country, such as an Ambassador, is not required to be summoned to the Foreign Ministry for every matter, whether it be to express pleasure or displeasure.

Instead of convening in person, a Note Verbale serves as an efficient means of conveying diplomatic messages or concerns. It holds a similar weight to verbal communication, effectively expressing the sentiments or positions of the sending government on various matters. Essentially, it is a formal note that carries the authority and significance of an oral message.

(f) Who is an Ambassador? An Ambassador is the highest-ranking diplomatic representative of one country to another country. They serve as the official liaison between their home country and the host country, representing their government's interests and promoting diplomatic relations. Ambassadors are typically appointed by their home government and are granted diplomatic immunity in their host country. They are responsible for conducting diplomatic negotiations, fostering cooperation, and addressing issues of mutual concern between the two countries. The official residence and office of an Ambassador is known as the Embassy, where they are accredited by the host country's government.

(g) Who is a High Commissioner?

The highest diplomatic representative from one Commonwealth country to another, operating from a mission known as the High Commission.

(h) Who is a Consul General?

The diplomatic representative at a sub-mission of a country, called the Consulate. The Consul General oversees a specific area of operation and reports to the Foreign Ministry of their country.

(h.1) Charge d'Affaires (CDA): The officer in a Diplomatic Mission responsible for managing the mission in the absence of the Head of Mission (Ambassador or High Commissioner).

(I) What is diplomacy?

The art of conducting foreign relations aimed at protecting the interests of the mother country; with the individual engaged in this process referred to as a Diplomat.

(j) Aide-memoire: An informal diplomatic message.

(k) Persona Non Grata (PNG): Refers to an undesirable person. If a member of a diplomatic mission engages in inappropriate activities, they can be declared PNG by the host state and must leave the country immediately or as specified.

(l) Diplomatic immunity: A principle of international law that exempts certain government officials and diplomats from the jurisdiction of local courts and authorities in the host country.

●●●

6

Experiences of Foreign Assignments : Karachi, Rome, Damascus, and Houston

My journey through various countries during my assignments with the Ministry of External Affairs has been enriching and transformative. Each posting brought unique experiences that shaped my understanding of culture, diplomacy, and global interconnectedness.

Karachi, Pakistan

My first posting in Karachi felt like stepping into another Indian city, save for the constant surveillance by local authorities. Surprisingly, I experienced no cultural shock. The city had a familiar vibe; we enjoyed watching Indian films on VCRs and were even fans of some Pakistani dramas. The legacy of Partition loomed over our interactions, reminding me of the shared history and culture that often transcends religious differences.

Despite the tensions and wars between our nations, I held onto the hope that peace could be fostered through dialogue and mutual understanding.

Rome, Italy

In Rome, I encountered a distinct cultural shock. The city was alive with history, and my family and I traveled to iconic places like Venice, Florence, and Pisa. Italians, still haunted by the memories of the World Wars, displayed a palpable sense of resilience. Living in a flat in a bustling marketplace, I was amused by an incident where a neighbor's towel fell onto our balcony. The ensuing conversation, facilitated by my daughter's unexpected grasp of Italian from cartoons, highlighted the interconnectedness of our lives.

The warmth and hospitality of the Italians were evident when a neighbor visited us, eager to try Indian tea, recalling fond memories from his time as a POW in India. My encounters with elderly war veterans in parks, who affectionately referred to Sikh soldiers as "molto bravo," added depth to my understanding of their history. The vibrant street life, with pizza shops and pubs filled with laughter and camaraderie, left a lasting impression.

Damascus, Syria

My assignment in Damascus introduced me to a different cultural landscape. The cost of living was incredibly low, and we often shopped for essentials in nearby Chhatura, Lebanon. A family trip to Beirut revealed the scars of war, with buildings riddled with bullet holes—a stark reminder of the country's turbulent past. Visiting the Dead Sea was a highlight; the buoyancy of the water was unlike anything I had ever experienced.

Life in Damascus was remarkably stable, with the army maintaining law and order effectively. Our time there was comfortable, and I appreciated the unique blend of history and modernity in the city.

Houston, USA

My final posting in Houston was a contrast to my previous experiences. The sheer scale of shopping malls was overwhelming, and the affordability of goods was surprising. An incident involving the return of a color TV showcased the efficiency of American consumer culture. When I attempted to return the TV due to voltage incompatibility, the store accepted it without question and, in a twist of fate, refunded more money than I had originally paid due to a diplomatic discount error. The staff's dedication to customer service left a lasting impression, even as we insisted on resolving the discrepancy fairly.

Living in Houston exposed me to a dynamic society where technology reigned, but I found myself reflecting on the potential downsides of such hyper-automation in our daily lives.

Conclusion

These experiences across Karachi, Rome, Damascus, and Houston have not only broadened my horizons but also deepened my understanding of cultural nuances and global relations. Each posting was a chapter filled with lessons, challenges, and unforgettable memories that I cherish to this day.

●●●

7

The World is Very Small

Once, during my posting at the Indian Embassy in Rome, I was working in the Visa and Passport Division. One day, while having lunch, our receptionist informed me that a visitor, Mr. Dangi, was in distress and requested to see me. Surprised, I asked him to come in. It turned out I knew Mr. Dangi, though he didn't recognize me. His younger brother had been a resident in my hostel back in India.

To break the ice, I asked if he was from Madina village in Rohtak district, a PhD from Haryana Agriculture University, and if his wife was the daughter of a Deputy Commissioner in Haryana. He confirmed all my guesses, visibly amazed at how I knew so much about him in a foreign land. I explained that I had met his brother during our hostel days.

Mr. Dangi explained his distress: he had come from an African country with a one-week stopover in Rome, planning to sightsee before returning to India. Unfortunately, while navigating a busy market, a thief had stealthily taken a small bag containing his passports, air tickets, credit card, and cash, leaving him with nothing. To make matters worse, he had locked his two children in their hotel room, giving the keys to the hotel manager. They hadn't eaten anything since the incident.

Understanding his plight, I ordered pizza for them and even secured permission from my office to take them to my official residence. They arrived on Monday, and after verifying their identities, we issued them limited validity passports and helped them retrieve their credit card.

On Friday evening, however, Mr. Dangi couldn't reach the Air India office in time due to delays in processing his credit card. I made a futile exercise to make the Air India official wait after hours to ensure Mr. Dangi received his tickets. Ultimately, Air India official told me that Mr. Dangi and his family would be issued air tickets on Saturday at Rome airport itself . I sent Mr. Dangi to RomeAirport four hours before his flight. Mr. Dangi and his family were issued air tickets by Air India at Rome Airport.

About three hours later, I received a jubilant call from him, letting me know that he was boarding his flight. I breathed a sigh of relief.

Fast forward 35 years later, while visiting Singapore with my wife, I met a couple named Sehrawat. During our dinner, he recounted an experience he had in Rome, where he had nearly fallen victim to a con man posing as a police officer. Smelling something fishy, he had entered a store and threatened to call real police, causing the con artist to flee.

Interestingly, he then shared an unhappy story about his brother-in-law who had a distressing experience in Rome but was saved by an Indian Embassy officer who had taken him in for a week. To his surprise, I revealed that I was that officer! Mr. Sehrawat then connected me with Mr. Dangi's wife, who was delighted to learn of our connection. She exclaimed, "The world is very small!"

This experience is just one of many where we, as embassy officials, helped Indian nationals in distress abroad. However, I feel disheartened by films like "Operation Airlift," which misrepresent the efforts of our embassy staff during crises, such as the evacuation of Indian citizens from Kuwait during the Iraq War. Our dedication and commitment to helping our compatriots should be accurately represented, reflecting the real stories of compassion and assistance that happen every day.

●●●

8

Sojourn to Australia

During my career, I had the privilege of traveling abroad multiple times, including visits to Ankara and Istanbul, and later to Cape Town. However, my most memorable trip was in 2017 when my wife and I traveled to Australia. This journey was not just about escaping the summer heat of India; it was a chance to connect with family and gain valuable insights into a different way of life.

Observations in Australia

Australia is remarkably vast—twice or thrice the size of India—yet its population is comparable to that of Delhi. This demographic contrast is striking. Everything in Australia is meticulously planned: there's no adulteration in food, fruits are naturally ripened, and the roads are impressively maintained. One of the most refreshing aspects was the cleanliness; people separate their waste diligently, and municipal trucks collect garbage weekly.

Despite these observations, I believe India has immense potential. If we can shed the colonial mindset that still pervades our society, I am confident we could elevate our status on the global stage. When the British arrived in India, we accounted for one-third of the world's GDP; now, that figure is around 6%. I firmly believe in the ingenuity and hard work of our people. With proper development and education, we could even surpass nations like China.

Challenges in India

However, India faces numerous challenges. A significant portion of the population remains illiterate and impoverished, and the quality of education often fails to prepare individuals for employment. Corruption is rampant, and many citizens evade taxes while accumulating wealth, often prioritizing dowries over education for their daughters.

To address these issues, we need to reform our mindset and approach to development. We should work towards quality education for all, ensuring that our young people are equipped for the job market rather than merely focusing on financial security through amassed wealth.

The Agricultural Crisis

Seventy percent of our population is engaged in agriculture or related activities, yet they remain burdened by debts. When farmers cannot repay their loans, they often resort to tragic measures, including suicide. During the 1965 famine, India faced immense challenges when both external threats and internal shortages threatened our food security. It was a time when Maharaja Patiala Sir Yadavendra Singh, our ambassador in Italy, rallied support from the Italian public, showcasing the solidarity of nations.

Our then Prime Minister, Lal Bahadur Shastri, famously proclaimed "Jai Jawan, Jai Kisan" to honor both our soldiers and farmers. This mantra resonated deeply, as it emphasized the vital roles these groups play in sustaining our nation.

A Call to Action

Today, our farmers still face severe challenges. They often sell their produce at prices dictated by middlemen while paying inflated prices for goods they need. The lack of proper storage facilities leads to significant food wastage reportedly estimated at ₹44,000 crores annually. This situation is heart-wrenching, especially when many in India go to bed hungry.

On a lighter note, during my time in Australia, I had the pleasure of meeting Vikas and Ritu Sheoran, who have gained recognition on YouTube and received the Haryana Pravasi Diwas award. I invited them for dinner and encouraged them to continue representing India positively abroad.

Conclusion

My experiences in Australia and my reflections on India remind me of the potential that lies within our country. With unity, a commitment to reform, and a focus on uplifting our farmers and marginalized communities, we can aspire to a brighter future. The journey is long, but with collective effort, we can indeed become the superpower we aspire to be.

●●●

9

My Love of Books

Books have always held a special place in my heart, serving as both companions and gateways to knowledge. When I was posted abroad, I securely stored my cherished collection of books and handwritten notes in a box at my wife's parental home in Bhiwani, Haryana. I had every intention of bringing them to Delhi when I finally settled into my own space. However, as fate would have it, my in-laws moved, rented out the house, and eventually, my beloved box was handed over to a relative.

To my dismay, I later learned that termites had invaded the box, devouring many of my precious volumes. Nobody wanted to keep the infested box, and it was discarded as waste. The loss felt monumental—I had lost what I considered my own libraries of Taxila and Nalanda, painstakingly built over the years.

A Heartfelt Connection

My love for books runs deep. During my tenure in Damascus, I frequently attended a book fair at the local library. One evening, I came across an encyclopedia that captivated me, but its price—US $400—gave me pause. For three days, I would lift it, contemplating its value. Finally, on the third day, the British bookseller encouraged me to make the purchase. I took the plunge and bought it, filled with joy that my daughters would benefit from this resource in their studies.

Another memorable experience involved an Indian man working with the UN peacekeeping force in Damascus. As he prepared to retire and move to New York, he put his collection of books up for sale. When he saw my enthusiasm, he was thrilled that someone was buying his books, and even offered some to me for free. I insisted on paying, but he sold me academic texts at incredibly low prices. This exchange underscored the immense value I place on books; my eldest daughter even received a certificate signed by the US President for her academic excellence—a proud moment that filled me with vicarious joy.

Building My Own Library

When my daughters completed their studies, I envisioned creating a mini-library in our home that would house both their books and mine. They often bring me books from abroad, knowing of my bibliophile tendencies. Even in retirement, I find solace and companionship in my books. My wife has embraced this aspect of my life, ordering books for me online and customizing an almirah in our covered balcony to keep them secure.

There was a time when she spent four months in Australia, yet I never felt lonely; my books provided all the company I needed. I genuinely believe that a book is a brain preserved in ink, and that a well-stocked book corner is the soul of a home. Recently, an idea struck me: to utilize my accumulated knowledge by teaching English and General Knowledge to students at a coaching institute, free of charge. This way, I can share the joy of learning that books have given me over the years.

●●●

10

My Mother and Her Wooden Sandook

In Haryana, it's customary for brides to receive a metal sandook filled with treasures from their fathers as part of their dowry. However, my mother's gift was a beautifully carved wooden sandook, a personal haven that held her world. As a child, I would watch her open it carefully, revealing new clothes, sweets, jewelry, dry coconuts and even money—each item a thread woven into the fabric of our family's story.

Despite my curiosity, my mother was a strict guardian of this treasure. She kept the sandook locked and seldom allowed me a peek inside. I learned to appreciate its mystery, knowing it was more than just a container; it was a symbol of her life and values.

I noticed that the sandook contained gifts—"tiwel"—that she would give to relatives on special occasions. Sometimes, those very gifts would return to her after years, passing through various hands, reflecting the deep bonds we shared as a family. Our community felt vast, as we typically married within a few select tribes, weaving a web of connections that made our family feel endlessly expansive.

As I grew older and began attending school in the city, donning western attire and adopting new manners, my mother softened a bit. She eventually allowed me to look inside the sandook, revealing her keen financial sense. Despite never having formal education, she managed our household with remarkable prudence. Our family never borrowed money; she preferred to save and invest wisely. When my brothers and relatives suggested buying a tractor with a bank loan, she declined, fearing the potential loss rather than the possible gain.

My mother's approach to money was straightforward: "Think five times before spending, and you will never feel poor." I took this advice to heart throughout my life, and it served me well. Our home was always abundant—filled with grains, milk, and desi ghee, a testament to her careful management.

Sadly, both my parents passed away many years ago, and now, our ancestral home stands empty, as my brothers have moved to their own farmhouses. Recently, I returned to the village for some repairs and found the exquisite sandook still in its place, now stripped of its treasures. The sight overwhelmed me, bringing back a flood of memories of my mother, who always envisioned me as a learned gentleman.

I remember when the opportunity arose for me to attend Lawrence School in Sanawar; the admission forms were brought, but my parents decided it was better to invest in all three of us rather than just one. They understood the value of education, a lesson I carry forward. I wish the same for my three daughters, encouraging them to pursue their studies wherever they may lead. Two have already graduated / post graduated and secured jobs, while the youngest is nearing the completion of her education.

The wooden sandook, now silent, stands as a testament to my mother's love, wisdom, and the legacy she imparted—a reminder of the importance of family, education, and financial prudence that continues to guide me.

Recently, I had the opportunity to visit my village to correct some land records at the tehsil headquarters. After successfully completing this task, I made my way to my ancestral home, eager to capture a photograph of the cherished wooden sandook that sparked such interest in my article. In particular, I wanted to honor the kind request from the former foreign Secretary Sujatha Singh, who expressed a desire to see this piece of family history.

While there, I uncovered new revelations from my eldest brother, who is now over 85 years old. I learned that my mother faced tremendous loss early in life; she lost both of her parents by the age of 10, leaving her to care for her baby sister. In her final moments, my grandmother entrusted my mother with the key to the wooden sandook, emphasizing the importance of looking after her sister.

At 18, my mother was married by the elder brother of her father since her father had passed away . She was gifted the wooden sandook, filled with precious gold (half a kilo) and silver jewelry (about five kilograms), along with other valuable items and clothing. Interestingly, she received 21 animals—camels, horses, buffaloes, and cows—as was the custom of the time.

Tragedy struck again when her sister, now married, also passed away. This series of losses left my mother in emotional turmoil. Yet, demonstrating remarkable resilience, she formed bonds with seven women in the village, whom she considered sisters. We affectionately called them "mausi," a term for real sisters. They rallied around her during difficult times, providing support, gifts, and wisdom.

My mother had a cousin but no real brother. During a pilgrimage to Haridwar with my father and other villagers, a man from a neighboring village offered to be her brother, as he had no sister of his own. They made a vow in the holy city, solidifying their bond.

Though my mother was not formally educated, she possessed an innate wisdom that helped her navigate life's challenges. The wooden sandook, a wedding gift to her mother in 1880, became her most treasured relic, symbolizing her lineage and the love of her deceased mother. It's clear now why she held such deep affection for this sandook and why she guarded its contents so closely, never allowing me a glimpse inside.

Unfortunately, the sandook has suffered from water logging in our home, leading to humidity that threatens its texture. I shared this concern with my wife and daughters, who live abroad. They unanimously insisted that we bring the sandook to Delhi for expert repairs, eager to preserve this piece of our family history.

This journey has deepened my understanding of my mother's attachment to the wooden sandook and her indomitable spirit in the face of adversity. I hope you find this emotional journey as meaningful as I do.

●●●

11

My Father and His Fears of Land Revenue Officials

As a small boy, I often found my father in a melancholy mood, a shadow of worry hanging over him. One day, driven by curiosity, I approached him and asked, "Why are you always so sad?" He placed his hand gently on my head and said, "When you grow up, become an officer, so you won't have to fear land revenue officials like I do."

At the time, I didn't fully grasp the weight of his words. It wasn't until years later that I understood their significance. Our first Prime Minister, Jawaharlal Nehru, had returned from a visit to the USSR in the late fifties with grand visions for Indian agriculture. Inspired by cooperative farming models he witnessed, he proposed a similar scheme for India: integrating all village lands for collective farming, supported by modern machinery. This initiative was met with widespread acclaim, but one voice stood against it—Chaudhary Charan Singh, a passionate leader from western Uttar Pradesh. His staunch opposition ultimately led to the repeal of the plan, averting potential chaos and bloodshed.

Though the scheme was retracted, it lingered in a modified form, aiming to consolidate individual farmers' lands. My father owned 84 acres spread across three separate parcels. The government's plan would disrupt our holdings, offering less fertile land in exchange, leaving my father at a loss. Fortunately, my educated brother-in-law stepped in, advocating for the preservation of our land's integrity. After a grueling ten-year battle, we regained our holdings.

Amidst this turmoil, my brother-in-law faced a personal crisis—his elder sibling fell ill with tuberculosis and was taken to a sanatorium in the Simla hills. While he sought admission for me at the prestigious Lawrence School, financial instability due to the land consolidation scheme meant we couldn't afford the tuition. The dream of attending that school faded as the pressing realities of our situation took precedence.

Fast forward to 2022, when my brothers and I found ourselves at the sub-tehsil office, hoping to correct some inaccuracies in our land records. Our file shuffled through various desks until it reached the Tehsildar's room. He scrutinized our Aadhar cards and files, but tension rose when our village Numberdar confronted him. As anger brewed, my younger brother's calm demeanor pacified the Tehsildar, and we agreed to provide the necessary affidavits to proceed.

In a moment of serendipity, I stood up to introduce myself. The Tehsildar's demeanor shifted; he rose to shake my hand, exuding warmth and assurance that the affidavits were merely procedural. As we navigated this bureaucratic maze, I couldn't help but recall my father's words. The fear that once overshadowed him had transformed into a moment of mutual respect and understanding.

Writing this anecdote serves as a therapeutic release, a way to confront and understand the demons of my past. My father's fears were not just his own but a reflection of the struggles many face within a complex system. Today, as I reflect on his hopes for me, I realize that my journey has been shaped by both his wisdom and the trials we endured as a family.

●●●

12

Four Pillars of My World : My Wife and Daughters

I previously mentioned that my wife and our three daughters as part of my nuclear family, but I feel that I should expand on this in greater detail to do justice to their importance in my life.

After being inducted into the Ministry of External Affairs, the time came for me to consider marriage. However, I had a condition: the bride must be a graduate. In those days, this was a high expectation, especially in my village. As a result, only one proposal came through where the bride met this requirement. Adding to the challenge, the custom in my village was quite orthodox; it was unheard of for a groom to meet his bride before the wedding. Nevertheless, I got married and began my new life with my wife in Delhi. It didn't take long for me to realize that I had found a learned, sophisticated, and highly organized partner.

Two years later, I received my first assignment abroad. People in my village had very little understanding of foreign postings. They knew that a few young men from a neighboring village had gone abroad for work and assumed that I was going abroad in a similar capacity. Even today, some of my relatives in the village still don't fully grasp the difference between going abroad for a government posting and going abroad for a private job. As they say, "ignorance is bliss" in my village.

During the journey of life, we were blessed with three daughters. They have all made their mark, living and working in some of the world's most bustling metropolises. They hold senior positions in multinational companies abroad, a success for which I credit my wife more than myself, as she played a pivotal role in grooming them. Two of my daughters hold MBAs from top international institutions, and the third has completed an exclusive leadership course from a prestigious school in the USA. I would like to share a small anecdote to highlight their brilliance.

When I was posted to Damascus, Syria, we were told that getting admission to the American School there was very difficult. It usually took a week for the school to decide, and it was common for students from the Embassy to be placed in a grade lower than their age group. With some trepidation, we took our daughters to the school for their admission tests. After some time, both of them walked past us with a teacher to another room. They whispered to us that they couldn't answer all the questions. However, the teacher, who had overheard their comment, assured us that they were given questions beyond their current level to assess if they could be placed in a higher grade. To our delight, not only were they admitted on the spot, but they were also placed in the appropriate grades. This came as a surprise to the Embassy staff, and our Ambassador, deeply impressed, praised our daughters' achievement on three different occasions in front of the entire staff.

One particular achievement of my eldest daughter stands out—she was honored with a U.S. President's certificate for excellence in her studies. Our youngest daughter, besides excelling academically, is also an exceptional dancer. When she was just five years old, she participated in a dance competition at Houston University Auditorium in the USA, competing against children in the 5-8 age group. She won first place and was awarded a $1,000 prize. She has also ventured into modeling, once modeling a Frontier Bazaar Lehenga at Neemrana Fort near Jaipur alongside actress Rimi Sen, known for her role in *Baghban* with Amitabh Bachchan.

My wife and I carefully strategized how to raise our daughters, choosing to be gentle and to avoid strict regimentation. An incident with my second daughter comes to mind. When she was just 3 or 4 years old, one morning she playfully grabbed both ends of my mustache. I asked her if she wasn't afraid of me, and with childlike innocence, she responded, "No." That moment encapsulated the kind of open, loving relationship we fostered with our children.

As I look back on my life, I realize that some people wronged me along the way. But instead of holding grudges, I learned from those experiences. I chose not to repay wrongs in kind and remained gentle with everyone, including my family. This approach, I believe, is one of the reasons for the success of my family members.

Books have always been my passion, and this love for reading rubbed off on my daughters. They became avid readers themselves, which built their confidence. So much so that I never had to worry about their futures or their ability to secure jobs—they did that with their own hard work and brilliance. Their accomplishments have made us proud parents, and seeing them rise in life brings us immense joy. From my humble beginnings in the small village of Mochiwali to their professional successes in global metropolises, it feels like we are living out some divine dream.

My daughters represent the essence of gender equality and women empowerment. We never imposed any limitations on them because they were girls; we encouraged them to pursue higher education both in India and abroad. In a country where son-preference runs deep, we feel no such longing. Our daughters' achievements have freed us from that mindset, and we have no regrets about not having a son.

In many ways, our daughters are our greatest source of pride and the realization of dreams we didn't even know we had.

●●●

13

The Legacy of Partition : A Dispassionate Reflection

The British Prime Minister Winston Churchill once reportedly remarked, "If you cannot hold India any longer, then divide it and quit." This directive was realized on August 14, 1947, when Mohammad Ali Jinnah succeeded in his scheme for Pakistan, leading to the emergence of two dominions: India and Pakistan.

Sir Cyril Radcliffe, an obscure lawyer unfamiliar with the subcontinent, was hastily summoned from London to delineate the borders of a nation he had never seen. The partition that followed resulted in tragic upheaval, with an estimated 10 to 20 million people crossing the newly drawn Radcliffe line. More than 2 million lives were lost, and countless women faced horrific acts of violence.

Historically, Hinduism and Islam had coexisted peacefully in India, a fact acknowledged even by the British colonial rulers. Muslim kings employed Hindu soldiers, while Hindu rulers had Muslim soldiers in their ranks. The unfortunate aberration of Partition marked the first time that Hindus and Muslims turned against each other on Indian soil. Notably, during the Third Battle of Panipat in 1761, the Maratha General Ibrahim Gardee's artillery devastated Ahmed Shah Abdali's forces, illustrating that religion alone should not dictate national boundaries. If it did, the creation of Bangladesh in 1971 would not have been possible.

India was united by a common history, geography, culture, and a composite civilization. We could have remained together. After the establishment of Pakistan, Jinnah famously declared that people were now free to go to their temples, mosques, and synagogues. This raises the question: why was the nation divided amid such bloodshed?

Upon the creation of Pakistan, Jinnah sent a signed letter to Maharaja Jodhpur—a Hindu-majority state—inviting him to merge with Pakistan on whatever terms he deemed appropriate. This raises doubts about the rationale behind the two-nation theory, which posited that Hindus and Muslims were inherently distinct nations. If communalism was indeed a significant issue, Partition failed to address it. Moreover, if the interests of Muslims were a genuine concern, why were the remaining Muslim minorities, further marginalized by Partition, left vulnerable under Hindu-majority rule?

The Muslim fear of Hindu domination often stemmed from misplaced anxieties. Jinnah initially rejected the Partition plan, calling it "mutilated, truncated, and moth-eaten." However, he ultimately accepted it when faced with the Viceroy's ultimatum: to accept the plan or risk losing everything. Jinnah had stirred such communal cauldron that he found himself compelled to embrace the very Pakistan he had once denounced.

Jinnah often boasted that he secured Pakistan with little more than the help of his secretary and her typewriter, suggesting he had not made any significant sacrifices. In reality, the personal costs of creating Pakistan were profound. Jinnah passed away in 1948 from tuberculosis, and his sister, Fatima Jinnah, struggled to find her place in the new political landscape. Meanwhile, Chaudhary Rahmat Ali, the proponent of Pakistan, returned from London after hearing news of the Partition and its accompanying chaos, only to find his parents in dire conditions at a refugee camp in Pakistan. He left without seeing them and ultimately died as a destitute and dejected figure, with his burial rites performed by the local council in London as an orphan.

A dispassionate evaluation reveals that Mohammed Ali Jinnah's actions ultimately marginalized the Muslims of the subcontinent, who now stand divided among India, Pakistan, and Bangladesh. The diverse faiths and belief systems that could have thrived under the umbrella of a composite culture, common civilization, shared history, and mutual geography have instead been lost, leaving us with a dream that sadly eluded realization.

●●●

14

Was There Justification for Dividing India and Pakistan Along Religious Lines in 1947?

This question merits serious examination based on my understanding of the subject. The term "Pakistan" was coined by Chaudhary Rahmat Ali in London in 1933 in his pamphlet Now or Never. The acronym stands for Punjab, Afghani (or Frontier Province), Kashmir, Sindh, and Balochistan. Notably, East Pakistan was reportedly not included in Ali's original vision.

Few are aware that the formation of Pakistan would have faced significant challenges had Sir Chhotu Ram been active in Punjab.

The Muslim fear of Hindu domination intensified following the provincial elections of 1937, where the Muslim League failed to secure a majority in any of the seven provinces. This defeat gave rise to the rhetoric for a separate Muslim state. Additionally, Indian representatives were not consulted when the country was drawn into World War II on the side of Britain. In 1939, the Congress ministries resigned at both the centre and provincial levels, a decision that the Muslim League celebrated as the "Day of Deliverance" on December 22, 1939. In hindsight, this resignation is viewed as a significant blunder, as it provided momentum to the demand for Pakistan.

Initially, the demand for Pakistan was not taken seriously, as every village, town, city, and metropolitan area in India had a Muslim population, making the feasibility of a separate state highly questionable. Mohammed Ali Jinnah emerged as the primary advocate for Pakistan, recognizing that he lacked political space within the existing framework. In 1940, he considered returning to London to pursue his legal career. Utilizing religion as an emotive issue, Jinnah successfully polarized the Muslim population to rally behind him, effectively politicizing religion.

Punjab, a crucial province, posed a significant obstacle to the creation of Pakistan. Sir Chhotu Ram, alongside Sir Fazal Hussain, formed the Unionist Party in 1923, which advocated for a united India. Until Ram's death on January 9, 1945, all 81 Muslim MLAs in Punjab were part of the Unionist Party, with even the two Muslim League MLAs aligning with them. Consequently, the prospect of Pakistan gaining traction in Punjab was virtually nonexistent.

It is documented that Sir Chhotu Ram managed to have Jinnah expelled from Punjab on March 10, 1944, a move orchestrated within 24 hours by the Premier of

Punjab, Sir KhijarHyat Khan, who took office on December 31, 1944, after the death of Sir Sikander Hayat Khan. Notably, there was no public outcry against Jinnah's unceremonious ouster from the Punjab, illustrating his lack of political support in Punjab.

On May 8, 1944, Sir Chhotu Ram organized a significant rally in Mianwali (now in Pakistan) to showcase his strength against Jinnah. Tragically, Ram passed away on January 9, 1945, leaving a void that Jinnah sought to exploit for his propaganda efforts in Punjab.

Sir Chhotu Ram had united farmers across religious lines—Hindu, Muslim, and Sikh—by aligning their economic interests. His popularity was such that he earned the honorific titles of "Rahbre Ajam" and "Deen Bandhu," or "Friend of the Poor." He also championed the "Agricultural Land Alienation Bill" in the Punjab Assembly, protecting farmers from exploitative moneylenders.

The Premier of Punjab, Sir KhijarHyat Khan Tiwana, became increasingly troubled by the activities of the RSS and the Muslim National Guard, leading him to impose a ban on them on January 25, 1947. The Muslim League and its leader, Mamdot, viewed Tiwana as a significant barrier to their goal of establishing Pakistan. An interesting anecdote recorded by Chaudhary Kewal Singh, ICS in his book, 'Partition and Aftermath' recounts how Ibrahim Khan Burke, the Minister of Education in Punjab, introduced his eight-year-old son to Tiwana. The child remarked, "Oh, he is that Tiwana uncle who is not allowing the formation of Pakistan." Distressed by this perception, Tiwana resigned from his position on March 2, 1947.

With the deaths of Sir Chhotu Ram and the resignation of Sir Tiwana, the path was cleared for Jinnah to intensify his campaign for Pakistan. During the Wavell Plan of 1945, the Unionist Party made a last-ditch effort to preserve national unity by requesting separate representation for Unionist Muslims in the Viceroy's Executive Council. However, the Viceroy hastily ended the meeting and the subject could not be discussed.

In Punjab, the Unionist government supported a united India. In the Frontier Province, there was a Congress government led by the legendary Abdul Gaffar Khan, and in Sindh, a coalition government comprised of the Muslim League and Hindu Mahasabha. Given these dynamics, there was little justification for dividing the subcontinent along religious lines. The lingering issues of our modern era can be traced back to the flawed logic behind this division.

Due to political instability, the 81 Muslim MLAs of the Unionist Party joined the Muslim League within six months of Sir Chhotu Ram's demise on January 9, 1945. He was a staunch advocate for farmers, having approved the "Bhakra Nangal Irrigation Project" on 08-01-1945 just one day before his passing away.

•••

15

Netaji Subhas Chandra Bose: A Legacy of Courage and Vision

Netaji Subhas Chandra Bose, born on January 23, 1897, in Cuttack, Orissa, remains one of India's most revered freedom fighters. His life was a remarkable saga of adventure, leadership, and relentless pursuit of independence. A true visionary, Bose's contributions to India's struggle for freedom are unmatched, and his story continues to inspire generations.

Bose was a man of extraordinary determination, known for his daring escapes from British imprisonment. Disguised as a Pathan, he managed to flee his house and travel to Kabul. From there, he ingeniously used an Italian diplomatic passport under the alias Orlando Mazzato to reach Russia, and later Vienna, where he sought an audience with Mussolini. Although he could not meet the dictator himself, he did connect with Mussolini's son-in-law, a significant figure in the Italian government.

His journey did not stop there. In Germany, Bose met Adolf Hitler to negotiate support for India's independence. Despite his request to have a derogatory remark about Indians removed from Hitler's book Mein Kampf, the meeting showcased Bose's audacity and commitment to his cause. Hitler eventually agreed to assist Bose and sent him towards the eastern theater of war.

In a dramatic twist of fate, Bose traveled on a Japanese submarine, accompanied by his Muslim friend Major Abid Hassan. With Japanese support, he raised the Azad Hind Fauj (INA), which aimed to liberate India from British rule. It's worth noting that the concept of an Indian National Army was initially inspired by King Mahendra Pratap who had previously raised an army in Kabul during World War I.

Under Bose's leadership, the INA achieved significant advances into India's northeastern regions. However, the tide turned with Japan's defeat following the atomic bombings of Hiroshima and Nagasaki in 1945, leading to the disbandment of the INA.

The circumstances surrounding Bose's death reportedly in a plane crash on August 18, 1945, remain shrouded in mystery, and despite numerous investigations, the truth has yet to be conclusively established. His enigmatic disappearance has fueled countless theories and discussions, ensuring that his legacy continues to be a topic of intrigue in India.

Netaji's impassioned call, "Give me blood, and I shall give you freedom," resonates deeply in the hearts of Indians, symbolizing his fervent desire for liberation. His vision of an independent India, where every citizen could thrive in dignity and freedom, is a guiding light for those who cherish national pride and self-determination.

In a nation rich with diverse histories, Bose's contributions stand out not only for their bravery but also for their profound impact on India's freedom struggle. His life reminds us that the quest for liberty often requires immense sacrifice and unyielding resolve. Netaji Subhas Chandra Bose's legacy is immortal, and his name will forever echo in the annals of Indian history. Jai Hind!

●●●

16

Deenbandhu Sir Chhotu Ram: A Legacy of Agricultural Reform and Unity

Deenbandhu Sir Chhotu Ram, born on November 24, 1881, in GarhiSampla, Rohtak district, emerged as a beacon of hope for distressed farmers in India. Originally named Ram Rachpal, he was affectionately known as "Chhotu Ram" or "little one" due to being the youngest among his siblings. His academic journey began at Saint Stephen's School in Delhi, where he excelled, passing his matriculation in 1901. He went on to earn a Bachelor of Arts from DAV College, Lahore, in 1905, standing out first in Sanskrit.

Chhotu Ram's life was profoundly influenced by the severe poverty faced by peasants, the teachings of the Arya Samaj, and his fervent desire for India's independence. His goal was to uplift the agrarian community through education and political empowerment. Inspired by the Bhagavad Gita, he initially worked as a private secretary to the Raja of Kalankar in Uttar Pradesh but soon left to pursue law studies in Lahore.

To fund his education, he taught at Rang Mahal High School and later shifted to Agra to join law college, graduating with distinction in 1911. He began his legal practice in Agra and then moved to Rohtak, where he also started the Jat Gazette, an Urdu weekly that became influential.

Chhotu Ram's writings in various publications created a stir in Punjab, inspiring educated discussions about farmers' rights and welfare. He joined the Indian National Congress and rose to become the President of the District Congress Committee. However, he left the party in 1920 due to differences with Mahatma Gandhi over the Khilafat Movement, which he believed would undermine farmers' interests.

His critique of the British judicial system was sharp and pointed; he famously remarked that winning a case often felt like a loss due to the delays, and losing a case felt like a death sentence. In 1923, he co-founded the Unionist Party with Sir Fazal Hussain, focusing on the needs of farmers.

Chhotu Ram was offered the position of Prime Minister of Kashmir State in 1927, but he declined, prioritizing the interests of farmers above personal ambition. As Minister for Agriculture and Industry, and later as Education Minister in 1924, he implemented numerous initiatives to improve agriculture and animal husbandry. He championed rural cooperative societies and village panchayats and promoted the study of agriculture and Unani medicine.

A significant aspect of his legacy is his fight against the exploitation of farmers by moneylenders. He actively addressed land alienation issues by strengthening the Land Alienation Act of 1900, giving it real enforcement power to protect peasants' rights.

Sir Chhotu Ram's life was dedicated to the upliftment of farmers and the pursuit of justice, making him a pivotal figure in India's socio-political landscape. His contributions, however, remain insufficiently recognized in the broader narrative of Indian history. His commitment and vision for agrarian reform continue to inspire those who advocate for farmers' rights today.

Deenbandhu Sir Chhotu Ram's legacy is deeply intertwined with the agricultural reforms he championed, particularly through legislation that safeguarded land ownership for the peasant castes in Punjab. According to this act, no land could pass from statutory landowning castes to non-agricultural castes like the Banias. The impact of this legislation was profound, as it significantly reduced the alienation of land, protecting farmers from fraudulent transactions and excessive indebtedness.

Chhotu Ram's efforts were instrumental in uniting Hindus, Sikhs, and Muslims, emphasizing their shared economic interests. His party, the Unionist Party, became a political force in Joint Punjab, maintaining a majority until his untimely death on January 9, 1945. His influence was palpable; the famous song "Jatta PagdiSambhal

Tera Lut Gaya Maal" resonated in Unionist meetings, symbolizing the agrarian struggle.

On May 8, 1944, just months before his death, Chhotu Ram organized a significant rally at Mianwali to challenge Mohammad Ali Jinnah's plans for Pakistan, rallying support from 81 Muslim MLAs in his party. His vision for unity among communities stood in stark contrast to the divisive rhetoric that Jinnah employed, which ultimately culminated in the creation of Pakistan on August 14, 1947. This partition, driven by communal passions, resulted in unimaginable human suffering, including the displacement of millions and the loss of countless lives.

Chhotu Ram's foresight was evident even in his final days. He signed the execution of the Bhakra Dam Project on January 8, 1945, a vision aimed at benefiting farmers across religions. His sudden passing left a significant void; farmers from all backgrounds mourned him, paying tribute to his contributions by honoring his successor, Khizar Hayat Khan.

The influence of Sir Chhotu Ram extended beyond Punjab. He inspired many, including prominent peasant leader NG Ranga from Andhra Pradesh. In contemporary India, as farmers face distress and rising suicide rates, Chhotu Ram's ideals and actions resonate more than ever.

Regrettably, he remains a largely forgotten hero in historical narratives. In Delhi, the absence of a road named after him stands in stark contrast to the recognition afforded to others. Chhotu Ram's legacy as a bulwark against communal strife and as a champion of farmers' rights continues to be relevant, reminding us of the importance of unity and social justice in times of division. Had he lived longer, his efforts might have significantly altered the course of history, potentially averting the Partition along religious lines.

Chhotu Ram's enduring influence is a call to remember the sacrifices made for agricultural reform and communal harmony in the Indian subcontinent. His life and work serve as a reminder of the ongoing struggle for farmers' rights and the necessity of fostering unity amidst diversity.

●●●

17

Could Sir Chhotu Ram Have Prevented the Partition of the Subcontinent?

Could Sir Chhotu Ram's untimely death on January 9, 1945, have altered the course of history and prevented the Partition of the subcontinent?

Mohammed Ali Jinnah had positioned himself as the principal advocate of Pakistan through his flawed "Two-Nation Theory," asserting that Hindus and Muslims were two distinct nations. This theory found few supporters, as many recognized the significant Muslim populations in every village, town, and city, questioning the practical viability of Jinnah's vision.

In contrast, Sir Chhotu Ram successfully united farmers of diverse faiths in Punjab—Hindu, Muslim, and Sikh—under a single banner. By integrating their economic interests, he founded the Unionist Party in 1923 alongside Sir Fazal Hussain. The Unionist Party championed the concept of one united nation, directly opposing Jinnah's divisive ideology.

When Jinnah began his propaganda efforts in Punjab, Sir Chhotu Ram took decisive action. On March 10, 1944, he orchestrated Jinnah's swift removal from the province, facilitated by Sir Khijar Hayat Khan Tiwana, the then Premier of Punjab. Notably, there were no protests in Punjab against Jinnah's eviction; he simply had no political traction there, as Punjab remained a significant obstacle to the formation of Pakistan.

On May 8, 1944, Sir Chhotu Ram demonstrated his strength by holding a massive rally in Mianwali (now in Pakistan) to counter Jinnah's influence. His earlier passage of the Agriculture Land Alienation Bill in 1900 fostered unity among farmers of different faiths, culminating in a sweeping victory for the Unionist Party in the 1926 elections. Even after his death, 81 Muslim MLAs remained aligned with the Unionist Party, and the two Muslim League MLAs also supported them.

The Unionist Party made a final attempt to keep the nation united during the Wavell Plan of 1945, advocating for separate representation for Unionist Muslims in the Viceroy's Executive Council. Unfortunately, the meeting was abruptly concluded by the Viceroy, stymying their efforts.

Following Sir Chhotu Ram's passing, Jinnah seized the opportunity to further his agenda in Punjab. In the ensuing political uncertainty, within six months, all Muslim MLAs from the Unionist Party defected to the Muslim League. Sir Chhotu Ram had stood as a formidable barrier against communal politics, and his presence may have prevented the violent fragmentation that followed, which resulted in the displacement of 10 to 20 million people and the tragic loss of over 2 million lives.

Sir Chhotu Ram was revered across religious lines in Punjab, earning him the honorific title "Rahbre Azam" or "Deenbandhu," meaning "friend of the poor." It is unfortunate that his contributions are often overlooked in Indian history. While places like Lawrence Road, Tolstoy Road, and Canning Road are prominent in Delhi, there is no road named after Sir Chhotu Ram.

When he passed away, farmers from various faiths traveled in bullock carts to his village of GarhiSampla near Rohtak, paying homage to the then Premier, Sir Khijar Hayat Khan Tiwana, and looking to him as their savior after the loss of Sir Chhotu Ram.

●●●

18

King Mahendra Pratap of Mursan

King Mahendra Pratap of Mursan, born on December 1, 1886, is a remarkable figure in India's struggle for independence, yet his contributions remain largely unrecognized in mainstream history. His deep commitment to freeing India from British rule drove him to unprecedented lengths, including traveling to 17 countries to seek support for the cause.

Often referred to as the "Marco Polo of India," Mahendra Pratap garnered significant international attention. He was granted a rare private audience with Kaiser William the Chancellor of Germany, before World War I, and received the prestigious Red Eagle award. His efforts culminated in the establishment of the Provisional Government of Independent India in Kabul on December 1, 1915, during the war. He also raised the Azad Hind Fauj in Kabul in 1929, receiving Afridi soldiers from King Habibullah Khan of Afghanistan.

Mahendra Pratap's commitment extended beyond military efforts; he launched the magazine World Federation to shed light on the atrocities of British rule, forming an executive board dedicated to India's freedom. In 1932, he was nominated for the Nobel Prize, but despite the lack of a satisfactory response to questions raised about his candidacy, he was denied this honor.

Notably, his influence extended to other prominent leaders, inspiring Netaji Subhas Chandra Bose to create a similar provisional government and military force. Upon returning to India in 1946, he first sought out Mahatma Gandhi instead of going directly to his home, reflecting his deep reverence for the freedom movement.

Mahendra Pratap's personal life was marked by his daughter, Bhakti Devi, who vowed to marry only when her father returned. Sadly, by the time he came back, she had passed the age of marriage and remained single her entire life, illustrating the strong bond between them.

In politics, Mahendra Pratap demonstrated his popularity by defeating Atal Behari Vajpayee in the 1957 Lok Sabha elections, having won previously in 1952 as well. However, despite his significant contributions, he has not received recognition commensurate with his impact on India's freedom struggle. The Indian government honored him with only a 30 paise postal stamp, and his legacy remains overshadowed.

He was a prolific writer and a learned individual, yet the British government confiscated his state in retaliation for his resistance. His contributions to the founding of Aligarh Muslim University are often overlooked in historical accounts. Mahendra Pratap passed away on April 29, 1979, and to date, no memorial exists in his honor.

Let us remember and honor King Mahendra Pratap, a true patriot whose bravery and dedication to India's freedom should inspire future generations.

●●●

19

India - China War of 1962

During my time in primary school, our teachers often reminded us of the national sentiment surrounding the India-China war. I vividly recall being asked to contribute one rupee to the National Defense Fund, highlighting the gravity of the situation. As Diwali approached, there was a somber tone in the air; many believed the festival should not be celebrated due to the ongoing conflict. As I grew older, I immersed myself in literature about the war, reading works like *Untold Story* by Lt. General B.M. Kaul, *Himalayan Blunder* by Brigadier J.P. Dalvi, and *India-China War* by Neville Maxwell, among others, to form my understanding of the events.

Based on my research, I share my perspectives on the war. Coinciding with the Cuban Missile Crisis, China launched its attack on India on October 20, 1962, reportedly shattering Jawaharlal Nehru's misguided 'forward policy' and leaving a lasting mark on India's military pride. Throughout the month-long conflict, strategic posts fell to the Chinese as India's military and political leadership faltered. Our junior officers and troops, ill-equipped in cotton uniforms and canvas shoes, fought valiantly, using bare hands and stones when ammunition ran out. In hindsight, the fall of Tawang, Walang, Se La, and Bomdila might have been avoided had India's commanders stood firm against the then-defence minister, Krishna Menon.

The root of the conflict lay in China's reportedly rejection of the borders established by the 1914 Simla Convention, which delineated Tibet's boundary between Aksai Chin in Ladakh and Xinjiang in the west, and NEFA (now Arunachal Pradesh) in the east. China sought to challenge this imperial legacy and bring India to the negotiating table. China refused to keep Tibet as a buffer . Nehru reportedly dismissed a boundary settlement proposed by Premier Zhou Enlai in 1960. This dismissal led Chairman Mao to decide to teach India a lesson, resulting in a devastating military defeat for India.

The Chinese initiated their offensive at Bum La and Thag La near Nam Ka Chu in the east, and Rezang La in Chushul in the west. Indian troops initially displayed commendable bravery. In the battle of Nam Ka Chu, the Rajput Battalion 2, under Brigadier Dalvi, fought valiantly but suffered heavy losses. Similarly, the 13 Kumaon Regiment, led by Major Shaitan Singh (posthumously awarded the Param Vir Chakra), defended Rezang La against seven Chinese assaults with remarkable tenacity. Overall operations in Ladakh were conducted under the adept command of Major General Budh Singh Dahiya, who executed his responsibilities with exceptional skill. The legendary Lata Mangeshkar articulated the grief of the nation due to the humiliating defeat at the hands of China through her famous song " ae mere watanke logo jarra ankh me bhar lo Pani ..." still makes every Indian lachrymose as it had made Pandit Jawahar Lal Nehru, when it was first sung on 26-01-1963, during the Republic Day function.

●●●

20

India - Pakistan War of 1965

When I was in primary school, the tensions of the India-Pakistan War of 1965 were palpable. I vividly recall the nights when Pakistani planes hovered over my village, creating an atmosphere of fear. One night, they dropped bombs near my village, Mochiwali, which thankfully fell harmlessly on sand dunes, resulting in minimal damage—just the loss of a buffalo and a few ruptured eardrums.

As I grew older, I immersed myself in literature to understand the complexities of the war. My perspective is shaped by several key observations:

Misjudgment by Pakistan: Pakistan believed that 1965 was the right time to seize Kashmir from India, underestimating India's military readiness and resilience.

Post-1962 Context: The Indian military was still reorganizing following its defeat by China in 1962. This defeat created a sense of vulnerability that Pakistan aimed to exploit.

Political Landscape: The death of Jawaharlal Nehru and the perceived ineffectiveness of his successor, Lal Bahadur Shastri, contributed to Pakistan's over confidence.

Socio-economic Issues: India was grappling with a food crisis and internal unrest, particularly anti-Hindi agitations in the South, which further led to the belief that India would not be able to mount a strong defense.

False Sense of Security: Pakistan's lack of diverse political discourse created an illusion of invulnerability, encouraging their military aggression.

Initially, Pakistan launched Operation Gibraltar, sending reportedly 5,000 infiltrators into Jammu and Kashmir to incite rebellion. However, this operation failed when India captured the strategic Haji Pir Pass, effectively cutting off the infiltrators' access.

As the war escalated, Pakistan reportedly shifted its focus to the Chamb-Jaurian sector, deploying 80 tanks and 10,000 troops. They briefly captured Khemkaran and Munabao railway stations, showcasing their advances through propaganda.

However, when Operation Gibraltar faltered, Pakistan initiated Operation Grand Slam. In response, India opened multiple fronts, defending its territory from Kargil to Kangerkot.

The conflict ultimately revealed the resilience of the Indian armed forces and led to a significant military and diplomatic response from India, reshaping the dynamics of the region. The war, though costly, underscored the necessity of preparedness and strategic foresight in the face of aggression.

In the early stages of the India-Pakistan War of 1965, a critical moment reportedly arose when General J. N. Chaudhary ordered Lt. General Harbaksh Singh, the General Officer Commanding (GOC) of the Western Command, to pull back and take a strategic position on the eastern side of the Beas River. However, to his credit, Lt. General Harbaksh Singh refused to comply with the withdrawal order. Instead, he led a bold counterattack against the advancing Pakistani forces.

This decisive action culminated in the Battle of Asal Uttar, near Amritsar, which became one of the largest tank battles since World War II. Under his leadership, Indian forces managed to destroy half of the Pakistani tanks in a single night. The bravery displayed in this battle earned Havildar Abdul Hamid a posthumous Param Vir Chakra, India's highest military honor.

Another significant engagement occurred in the Chawinda-Philora sector, where Indian troops advanced to within 4,000 yards of Sialkot. Led by the legendary Brigadier Khem Karan Singh, who hailed from a distinguished Jat family in Rohtak, Haryana, the Indian forces successfully destroyed 80 Pakistani tanks. For his extraordinary courage, Brigadier Khem Karan Singh, later Lieutenant General, was awarded the Maha Vir Chakra, the nation's second-highest award for gallantry.

On September 10, 1965, Indian forces captured the Pakistani township of Barki, located 15 miles southeast of Lahore. Lt. Colonel Hari Singh of the Tiger 18 Cavalry, later promoted to Brigadier, had the honor of hoisting the Indian flag at the Barki police station, marking a significant victory for Indian forces during the conflict.

Another significant engagement during the India-Pakistan War of 1965 took place at Dograi. Initially captured on September 6, the position had to be vacated due to a lack of reinforcements. However, the 3rd Jat Battalion later advanced to the outskirts of Lahore, on the night of September 20-21 , but had to withdraw following the ceasefire declaration on September 23.

The Battle of Dograi stands out as one of the most brutal in Indian military history, resulting in the deaths of 86 Indian soldiers and 308 Pakistani soldiers. During the fierce combat, Indian forces captured Pakistani Commander Colonel Golwale along with his battery commander, two additional officers, five Junior Commissioned Officers (JCOs), and 108 Pakistani soldiers. The intensity of this battle earned the 3rd Jat Battalion numerous honors: 4 Maha Vir Chakras, 4 Vir Chakras, 7 Sena Medals, 12 mentions in despatches, and 11 Chief of Army Staff (COAS) commendation certificates. This battle immortalized Colonel (later Brigadier) Desmond Hayde, his junior officers, and the brave soldiers under his command.

Retired Air Marshal Asghar Khan, a Pakistani author of the war reportedly , acknowledged in his book "The Second Round" that the conflict ended in a stalemate, with both sides claiming victory. However, it was clear that India had delivered a significant blow to Pakistan.

The war concluded with the Tashkent Agreement in the USSR, which sought to restore peace between the two nations.

Tragically, Prime Minister Lal Bahadur Shastri passed away on January 11, 1966, shortly after the conflict. He had famously championed the slogans "Jai Jawan, Jai Kisan." During this time, China refrained from coming to Pakistan's aid, instead sending a note to India urging the dismantling of Indian defenses in Sikkim.

The culmination of Pakistan's mischief began in September 1965 and ultimately led to its dismemberment on December 16, 1971, when 93,000 of its soldiers and civilians surrendered to Indian forces.

●●●

21

India - Pakistan War of 1971

During my college years, the atmosphere was charged with the impending war between India and Pakistan. As I began reading English newspapers, I followed the developments closely, particularly the tense moments when the US 7th Fleet entered the Bay of Bengal, causing nationwide anxiety. However, this passed without incident. My extensive reading on the subject led me to formulate my understanding of the war.

On March 17, 1971,Mrs. Indira Gandhi was sworn in as Prime Minister for a third time, having consolidated her power within the Congress Party and the country. Just eight days later, a major crisis erupted in what was then East Pakistan. The geographic divide between East and West Pakistan had long been a source of tension, described by Salman Rushdie as "a bird with two wings but no body." The two regions shared little beyond their Islamic faith, and deep-seated linguistic and cultural differences were exacerbated by the West Pakistani military's oppressive rule.

Field Marshal Ayub Khan's treatment of the East was particularly brutal, culminating in the imprisonment of the charismatic leader Sheikh Mujibur Rehman. His successor, Yahya Khan, continued this oppression. In the 1970 general elections, the Awami League, led by Rehman, secured a landslide victory in East Pakistan, while Z. A. Bhutto's Pakistan Peoples Party claimed a majority in the West. However, the Bhutto-Yahya nexus denied Rehman the premiership, sparking a significant backlash. When Rehman declared East Pakistan's independence on March 25, 1971, Yahya Khan's military responded with a severe crackdown, resulting in widespread atrocities.

As refugees fled to India in droves, Indira Gandhi embarked on a world tour to highlight the crisis. Public sentiment in India shifted toward intervention. Army Chief Sam Manekshaw advised against immediate action, advocating for preparation. Despite the party line suggesting that the Mukti Bahini, the rebel forces of East Pakistan, could prevail on their own, the situation remained dire.

The geopolitical landscape was complex, with Nixon and Kissinger opposing India, and the US making it clear they would not support India should China intervene. In response reportedly , India signed a peace treaty with the USSR, which deployed troops along the Sino-Soviet border, sending a strong message. Despite the US Seventh Fleet's presence, Indira Gandhi maintained her composure, prompting Atal Behari Vajpayee to liken her to the goddess Durga.

The war officially began on December 3, 1971, with Pakistan's preemptive air strikes against Indian airfields. Major General JFR Jacob, Deputy Chief of Staff of the Eastern Command, sought to negotiate Pakistan's surrender with General AAK Niazi. After repeated requests, Niazi agreed to surrender, leading to a historic moment on December 16, 1971, when he signed the Instrument of Surrender before Lt. General Jagjit Singh Aurora, GOC eastern command, marking the largest military capitulation since World War II.

Ultimately, India emerged victorious, with 93,000 Pakistani soldiers and civilians surrendering. However, the subsequent Simla Agreement saw India return these prisoners of war without securing a favorable arrangement, reflecting a missed opportunity in the policy-making process. This war not only reshaped the political landscape of South Asia but also highlighted the complex interplay of regional and international politics during a turbulent time.

●●●

22

The Battle of Dograi - the fiercest battle in the military history of India, during the India - Pakistan War of 1965.

The Battle of Dograi, during the India-Pakistan War of 1965, stands as one of the fiercest engagements in India's military history. Dograi, located on the east bank of the Ichhogil Canal near the Grand Trunk Road, was critical for controlling access to Lahore.

On September 6, 1965, the Indian Army crossed the international border near Wagah, killing 35 Pakistani soldiers and capturing many more. Despite heavy Pakistani airstrikes, 3 Jat successfully took the east bank of the Ichhogil Canal and advanced south to capture Dograi, a fortified township near Lahore, through intense fighting. However, due to lost communication with Brigade headquarters and lack of artillery support, Indian forces were forced to hold their positions for eight days. During this time, Pakistan fortified Dograi with reinforcements, leading to a tactical retreat by Indian forces.

India then planned a two-phase offensive to recapture Dograi. While 13 Punjab of the Indian army achieved limited success, the pivotal assault was led by the tenacious Lt. Colonel Desmond Hayde of 3 Jat, who launched a daring night attack on September 20-21. Despite being outnumbered and facing a Pakistani tank squadron, 3 Jat surprised the enemy and engaged in grenades, guns, and bayonet attack which ultimately turned into fierce hand-to-hand combat. Against the odds, they captured Dograi,with a loss of 86 of its brave hearts, killing 308 Pakistani soldiers and capturing key officers - commanding officer Golwale, his battery commander, 2 more officers, 5 JCOs and 108 soldiers.

The bravery of 3 Jat was recognized with numerous honors, including 4 Mahavir Chakras and 4 Vir Chakras, 7 Sena medals, 12 mentions in dispatches, 11 COAS commendation cards. Despite this victory, Indian forces were ordered to pull back following the ceasefire on September 23, 1965. The Battle of Dograi remains a testament to Indian military prowess, though it is also seen as a missed opportunity to decisively end the conflict with Pakistan.

●●●

23

Jammu & Kashmir : A Historical Overview

With the dawn of Independence on August 15, 1947, British paramountcy over the 565 princely states came to an end. These states were given the choice to join either India or Pakistan. While most states promptly joined one of the two nations, Jammu & Kashmir, Hyderabad, and Junagadh hesitated.

Maharaja Hari Singh of Jammu & Kashmir dithered on the decision. However, before he could finalize his stance, Pakistan launched an aggressive invasion aimed at annexing the territory. In response to this external threat, the Maharaja signed the Instrument of Accession to India, thus transforming the conflict into one of national significance. Indian troops were deployed to repel the Pakistani forces, but they halted just five miles short of Srinagar, the state's capital.

India succeeded in reclaiming certain areas, but Prime Minister Jawaharlal Nehru, advised by then-Governor General Lord Mountbatten, took the issue to the United

Nations. This led to a prolonged stalemate in the UN, with Pakistan continuing to assert its claim over Jammu & Kashmir. The region has since witnessed multiple military confrontations, including attacks by Pakistan in 1948, 1965, 1971, and 1999.

Today, approximately one-third of Jammu & Kashmir remains under what is referred to as Pakistan Occupied Kashmir (POK). The demarcation between India and Pakistan, initially called the ceasefire line following the 1965 war, evolved into the Line of Control (LoC) after the 1971 conflict.

In a significant political shift, the Indian government passed the Jammu & Kashmir Reorganization Act in 2019, effective from October 31 of that year. This act abrogated Articles 370 and 35A, which had conferred special status upon the region, and bifurcated it into two Union Territories: Jammu & Kashmir and Ladakh.

This reorganization is seen by many as a potential new dawn for peace and stability in Jammu & Kashmir and Ladakh. As the region moves forward, the hope is that lasting solutions can be found to ensure harmony and development for all its residents.

●●●

24

Maharaja Surajmal Misrepresented : Setting the Record Straight on Bollywood's 'Panipat'

It is disheartening to see that Indian history has often overlooked some of our national heroes, a trend that extends even to Bollywood portrayals. One glaring example is the depiction of Maharaja Surajmal in the film Panipat. Despite public protests leading to the removal of some scenes, the portrayal of Maharaja Surajmal as a corpulent, comical figure speaking in a strange dialect is both inaccurate and disrespectful.

Maharaja Surajmal was a vigorous and skilled king, renowned for his ambidextrous swordsmanship on the battlefield. His wisdom earned him the title of "Jat Plato" among historians. When Ahmed Shah Abdali demanded a hefty tribute, Surajmal cleverly deflected the demand by writing a diplomatic letter, stating he was not a king but a significant zamindar. He argued that if Abdali attacked, it would highlight his own weakness by forcing a mighty king to battle a zamindar. He confidently declared that the forts of Deeg and Bharatpur would withstand any siege, fortified by strategic designs that rendered them nearly invulnerable.

The unique construction of his forts—designed with a sand and mud barrier—ensured that no artillery of the time could breach their defenses. This made it clear why Abdali chose not to engage Surajmal.

In 1761, Surajmal did bring a formidable force to assist the Marathas in the Third Battle of Panipat, but his advice on guerrilla tactics was dismissed by the overconfident Maratha General Sadashiv Rao Bhau. As a result, Surajmal refrained from participating in the battle. After the Marathas faced a devastating defeat, he extended his protection to their survivors, spending a substantial amount to ensure their safety and escorting them back to Maharashtra. This act of compassion led to a warm welcome for Jat soldiers, who were granted land and opportunities to marry into Maratha families, thereby forming a new societal bond . The emergence of 22 Jat villages over a time in Malegaon tehsil of Nasik district of Maharashtra is testimony to the Jat- Maratha matrimonial alliance.

Unfortunately, these significant aspects of Maharaja Surajmal's legacy were not depicted in the film. It is crucial that we present history with integrity, avoiding embellishments and misrepresentations. Our heroes deserve a portrayal that reflects their true valor and contributions, and it is essential to honor their legacies with accuracy.

●●●

25

Exploring My Roots

In 1995, during my home leave from Damascus, I visited our farmhouse in Haryana instead of our ancestral home in Mochiwali, as my brothers had moved there after our parents' passing away. One afternoon, while napping in the guest room, I was startled awake by a loud thud. A man had entered, carrying a load that resembled accounting books, typically used by Marwari Banias. He introduced himself as our genealogy chronicler from Rajasthan.

Initially, I regarded him with disdain and skepticism, but curiosity soon took over. I asked him about the origins of the Jats. He claimed we descended from Rajputs. While I personally disagree, I chose not to engage in any polemical argument. Historically, Jats were invited to Mount Abu during invasions and ceremonially rechristened as Rajputs through sacrificial fire, leading to the emergence of the Chahuman or Chauhan Rajputs from 24 Jat clans.

According to the priest, the notion of our descent from Rajputs arose during the Mughal era when many Jats, having taken on the Rajput identity, eventually returned to their original Jat roots because being a Jat was not a social disability. This transition reportedly angered the Rajputs, who decreed that only Rajputs and Brahmins could draw water from village wells. This edict deeply offended Jats, particularly the Dhaka Jats of Churu district, leading to a violent confrontation where many lost their lives.

A poignant story from this conflict involves a Chahar woman, married to a Dhaka, who reached the battlefield three days later from her parental home in a far away village. Despite her desire to die for her fallen kin, she was persuaded not to, as she was pregnant. She gave birth to a posthumous son, christened "Julia," a Rajasthani term meaning "child born after the death of a father " or posthumous child .Julia proved to be enterprising, founding the city of Juliasar, which still exists today. As a mark of respect, we do not marry a Chahar woman because Julia was born to a Chahar woman.

My family traces its lineage to Julia, with connections to royalty. One notable ancestor was Raja Kanak Singh Dhaka, whose realm was later absorbed into the Mughal empire. Additionally, a Subedar or Governor named Rao Jasraj Singh Dhaka had ties to our clan. My forefathers initially lived in Sidhmukh near Rattangarh before migrating to Mochiwali. They first settled in Kharia village in the 18th century but later moved to Mochiwali, acquiring agricultural land with the advantage of irrigation from a canal built in 1899-1900. Our land in Kharia was lost to unscrupulous individuals while my father's uncle served in World War I.

The history of the Dhaka Jats, their identity shifts, and resilience highlight a rich legacy that deserves recognition and celebration.

●●●

26

How the Idea to Write the History of Jats Came About

During my posting in Karachi, Pakistan, I had an experience worth sharing: one day, I noticed an officer from the mission writing about Indian history. When I entered his room for some official business, I found him dictating notes on the "Hun" invasion. He mentioned that the Huns could not withstand the heat of India and eventually left, while those who stayed integrated into the Indian population. Curious, I asked him who they might be today, and he suggested they could be the "Jats."

As a Jat myself, I was taken aback, as I didn't see any of the traits , he had described, in myself. This sparked my quest to understand the Jats more deeply. I conducted extensive research on their history both in India and abroad. My findings are detailed in my comprehensive essay " The Jats : A Saga of Valor, Heritage and Resilience".

I came across an intriguing anecdote: "Unpadh Jat Padhe brabar aur Padha Jat Khuda brabar," meaning "An uneducated Jat is equal to an educated person, but an educated Jat is equal to God." While it may be apocryphal, it is prevalent in folklore.

In this story, a man left a will stipulating that half of his property should go to his first son, a quarter to his second son, and one-fifth to his third son. The estate consisted of 19 horses, and no one could figure out how to divide them according to the will. The case eventually reached the Muslim King Balban, but even he was unable to resolve it.

It was reportedly the famous traveler Amir Khusro who suggested referring the matter to the Jats, known for their expertise in delivering judgments through their Khap Panchayats.

An errand was sent to the Jat Khap headquarters in Muzaffarnagar, where Chaudhary Ram Sahay Jat rode to the King's court. He requested that all 19 horses be brought outdoors. Chaudhary Ram Sahay asserted on the premise that all state property belonged to the king and asked for permission to add his own horse to the mix, bringing the total to 20 horses.

He then distributed the horses: 10 to the first son (half), 5 to the second son (a quarter), and 4 to the third son (one-fifth). In this clever way, Chaudhary Ram Sahay Jat managed to divide all the horses according to the will and took his horse back with the King's approval.

The onlookers erupted in joy, chanting, "Unpadh Jat Padhe brabar aur Padha Jat Khuda brabar," meaning that an uneducated Jat is equal to an educated person, while an educated Jat is equal to God.]

●●●

27

The Jats: A Saga of Valor, Heritage, and Resilience

Jats are an identifiable community of Indo-Aryan descent known for their tall, sturdy, and strong physique. They are recognized as industrious and adventurous individuals. Although their religious beliefs and practices may vary, Jats predominantly inhabit regions in present-day Pakistan, Punjab, Haryana, western Uttar Pradesh, and Rajasthan.

Regardless of whether they identify as Hindu, Muslim, or Sikh, Jats across these areas share similar social customs. The Jat community is not only celebrated for being among the finest peasantry in the subcontinent but has also produced valiant warriors, poets, patriots, great administrators, eminent scholars, saints, and sages throughout history.

Those who have migrated from Hinduism to Sikhism or Islam typically do not emphasize their previous caste. However, those who transitioned from Hindu Jat to Sikhism or Islam often take pride in their Jat identity, identifying themselves as Jat Sikh or Jat Muslim. Former

Foreign Minister Shri K. Natwar Singh reportedly notes in his book *Maharaja Surajmal* that "being Jat is a status symbol."

Indian history can be divided into three distinct periods:

1. Ancient/Hindu or Buddhist Period
2. Muslim or Medieval Period
3. Arrival of the British or Modern Period

In the Ancient/Hindu or Buddhist period, the rulers included many prominent Jat leaders, a fact that is likely to gain wider acceptance over time.

One notable Jat king from this era was Yasodharman Virk, who ruled Malwa (present-day Madhya Pradesh) from 528 to 543 AD. He is remembered for eliminating the Hun and Saka threats in India.

Another significant figure was Maharaja Harsh Vardhan Bains, a powerful Jat king who reigned from 606 to 640 AD. Following his death, India fragmented into small princely states, resembling a jigsaw puzzle.

Jats are not just a phenomenon of the 18th century, when they established their own rule around Mathura and its surrounding areas, defying the Mughal Empire. In fact, Jats have an ancient and rich history. They originally inhabited regions along the borders of Iran and Afghanistan, forming large tribes that eventually evolved into present-day Khaps, with their tribal councils known as Khap Panchayats.

Jats reportedly date back to the time of the Mahabharata War, around 3102 BC. They are true sons of the soil, having consistently defended their motherland against foreign aggression. As they worked in the fields to feed the nation, they were always prepared to protect it with their lives.

As reportedly noted by Shri K. Natwar Singh in his book *Maharaja Surajmal*, "Jats kept their gaze at the ploughshares , but when the right opportunity came, they turned their ploughshares into swords."

The rule of Sindh under the Jat King Shahsi Ray was reportedly usurped by his Brahmin priest, Rai Chach, who assassinated the king and seduced his wife.

In 1957, Marshal Zhukov, a legendary commander of the former Russian army, addressed cadets at the Indian Military Academy in Dehradun, stating that Alexander never actually defeated the Indian king Porus in the famous battle of Hydaspes (Jhelum) in May 326 BC, challenging a common misconception.

To prevent foreign invasions from the northwest, Brahmin priests reportedly invited the Jats to Mount Abu, intending to rechristen them as Rajputs without the stipulation of treating Brahmins as superior in the Hindu hierarchy. However, once the Jat clans assembled, the Brahmins reversed their position and insisted on their superiority. Some Jat clans returned in protest, but from those who remained, the Chahuman or Chauhan clan emerged from the 24 Jat clans.

Mahmud Ghazni reportedly launched a series of attacks on India from 1001 AD to 1027 AD, with his final assault in 1027 AD aimed at punishing the Jats of Sindh for harassing him during his raids.

In 1191 AD, Prithvi Raj Chauhan defeated Mohammed Ghori in the first battle of Tarain, but in the second battle in 1192 AD, Ghori emerged victorious. The Jats, however, did not remain passive; they organized resistance under the leadership of Jatwan Malik Jat, besieging the fort of Hansi and preventing the Muslim commander from emerging. This situation compelled Qutubudin Aibek to personally march against the Jats.

A fierce and bloody conflict ensued, resulting in heavy casualties on both sides. After several days of fighting, Jatwan Malik suffered martyrdom, marking the end of organized Jat resistance.

The Khokhar Jats defeated Mohammed Ghori in 1205 AD at Jhelum, but he retaliated and defeated them in 1206 AD. However, on his way back to Ghazni, he was assassinated by the Khokhar Jats at a place called Dhamiak near Multan.

The first Muslim female ruler of Delhi, Razia Sultan, who reigned from 1236 to 1240 AD, sought the help of the Jats to regain her throne after being deposed by her enemies.

Jats reportedly also served as mercenary soldiers in the Middle East and Russian republics. Some became trapped in Transoxiana (modern-day Uzbekistan) and, unable to return, converted to Islam, the dominant religion of the region, and became rulers known as Jat Khan. Tamarlane, a general under Jat Khan, conspired with his brother-in-law to assassinate him. The son of Jat Khan fought against Tamarlane but was unsuccessful.

When Tamarlane invaded India in 1398 AD, the Jats seized the opportunity to return to India, but they did not fight for him. After a period of transition through Buddhism, they reconverted to Hinduism.

In the Russian language, "Jat" reportedly signifies headstrong, intrepid, or desperado.

During the reign of Delhi Sultan Allauddin Khilji (1296 AD to 1316 AD), the standard land revenue was increased from one-sixth to an astonishing 50%. In response, all the Jat Khaps convened at the Jat Khap Panchayat headquarters in Muzaffarnagar. They unanimously decided not to pay any taxes, fully aware that this decision would invite punitive action from the Sultan.

When the Sultan launched an attack with 30,000 soldiers, the Jats mustered 28,000 youths and decisively defeated his forces. The Sultan was forced to humble himself, sue for peace, and even paid war reparations to gain Jat support against potential foreign invasions from the north.

In 1398 AD, Tamarlane invaded India, and the Khokhar Jats boldly challenged him. However, they were significantly outnumbered and suffered defeat. Many Jats became martyrs, while others were captured and subjected to genocide. Yet historians reportedly note that "still the high Jat spirit did not suffer any diminution."

The rule of Jat King Pandu Singh Godara of Jangle Desh was reportedly usurped by Rajput prince Rao Bika of Jodhpur, in connivance with Brahmin priests, in 1486 AD. This led to the renaming of the state as Bikaner.

It is documented that 5,000 Jat soldiers fought alongside Rajput King Rana Sanga in the Battle of Khanwa in 1527 AD. In the Second Battle of Panipat in 1556 AD, Jats under Hemu Jat challenged Mughal King Akbar but were ultimately defeated. Contrary to common belief, which claims Hemu was from the business community or Bania, he was, in fact, a Jat chieftain as noted in pages 259-260 of *Mughal Empire in India* by British historian Sir Edward Sullivan. In a twist of fate, Hemu was gaining the upper hand when an arrow struck his eye, causing confusion among his troops and leading to their defeat.

In 1660 AD, Jats in the Agra region revolted under the leadership of Gokula Jat. The intensity of the uprising forced Mughal King Aurangzeb to relocate his capital from Delhi to Agra in 1667 AD out of fear of the Jats. Several Jat heroes challenged Mughal authority, but Maharaja Surajmal firmly established himself as a key figure. His influence was so significant that no Mughal king could ascend the throne in Delhi without his permission.

Maharaja Surajmal arrived with a large force to assist the Marathas in the Third Battle of Panipat in 1761 AD, but he did not participate in the battle due to the disregard shown by Maratha General Sada Shiv Rao Bhau for his advice on guerrilla warfare. After the Marathas suffered defeat, Maharaja Surajmal offered protection to Maratha men, women, and children in his forts, providing a large escort of Jat soldiers to help them return safely to Maharashtra.

The grateful Marathas honored the Jat soldiers with a grand welcome, offering them land to settle and permission to marry Maratha women and war widows . Over time, 22 Jat villages were established in the Malegaon tehsil of Nashik district, Maharashtra.

Ahmed Shah Abdali demanded a substantial sum of money from Maharaja Surajmal, who diplomatically refused by stating that he was not a king but a significant zamindar. He warned that if Abdali attacked, his forts at Deeg and Bharatpur would be as invincible as the ramparts of Alexander. Abdali chose not to pursue the attack on Maharaja Surajmal.

Maharaja Surajmal's son, Maharaja Jawahar Singh, later prevented Ahmed Shah Abdali from plundering the Hindu holy site of Mathura. With the help of his brave Jat soldiers, he engaged in a fierce conflict that resulted in heavy casualties on both sides.

Jats played a significant role in the First War of Independence in 1857 AD. Notable figures included Jat King Nahar Singh of Ballabgarh, Raja Bahadur Singh Thakran of Gurgaon, Raja Amani Singh of Aligarh, Raja Mohan Singh of Shamli, Raja Dev Singh of Mathura, Jat Raja Daya Karan Singh Hegga of Sadabad, Jat Raja Shahmal Tomar of Baghpat, and Chaudhary Ram Singh of Balla village in Karnal. All of these leaders suffered martyrdom during the uprising, which led to the disbandment of Haryana state in 1858.

Two young Jat sisters from Barot, Uttar Pradesh—Shiv Devi, age 16, and Jai Devi, age 14—also participated in the First War of Indian Independence.

The Battle of Saragarhi on September 12, 1897, saw 21 Jat Sikh soldiers hold out against 12,000 Afghan tribesmen, inflicting heavy casualties until all 21 soldiers were martyred.

Jat King Mahendra Pratap of Mursan established the first provisional government of Independent India and founded the first Azad Hind Fauj in Kabul during World War I.

Sir Chhotu Ram advocated for the Agriculture Land Alienation Bill in the Punjab assembly to protect farmers from moneylenders.

Dayal Singh Majithia Shergil Jat (1848–1894) founded the Punjab National Bank, *The Tribune* newspaper, and Dyal Singh College in Lahore.

Philanthropist Chhaju Ram opened schools in the Jat heartland, furthering education in the community.

Jat soldiers predominantly served in both World Wars reportedly to establish peace and order. Estimates reportedly suggest that around 80% of the soldiers who fought in these wars were Jats. They defended Palestine against Turkish forces during World War I, and the grateful locals named villages after Jat soldiers, which now fall in Israel.

The 6th Jat Light Infantry suffered heavy losses in 1915 during a horrific campaign in France in World War I.

Field Marshal Sir Claude Auchinleck, deployed at the Burma front during World War II, remarked, "If things looked bleak and danger threatened, I would ask nothing better than to have Jat soldiers beside me in the face of the enemy."

According to *Appleton's Journal* (Vol. 15, Issue 379, New York, June 24, 1876), it was noted that "no Hindoo race more heroically resisted the invasions of the Mohammedans." The Jats notably confronted Mahmoud on the Indus, and Tamarlane could only conquer their legions by utterly destroying them.

Jat soldiers demonstrated their bravery in several wars against Pakistan in 1948, 1965, 1971, and 1999. During the Kargil operation, of the reportedly 471 casualties, 322 were Jats, with 171 from Haryana alone.

On the night of September 20-21, 1965, during the India-Pakistan war, 3 Jat Regiment of the Indian Army captured the Pakistani township of Dograi, on the outskirts of Lahore. This fierce battle resulted in the loss of 86 Indian soldiers while inflicting significant casualties on the enemy, including 308 Pakistani soldiers and the capture of Pakistani Commanding Officer Golwale his battery commander along with two other officers, five Junior Commissioned Officers, and 108 soldiers.

The intensity of the battle is reflected in the accolades awarded to the 3 Jat Regiment: 4 Mahavir Chakras, 4 Vir Chakras, 7 Sena Medals, 12 mentions in dispatches, and 11 COAS commendation cards.

At the dawn of Independence on August 15, 1947, there were 565 princely states in India, of which 84 were Jat states. Among the 12 Misals or ruling Khaps in Punjab, 9 belonged to the Jats.

Shri Tara Singh Ji Rajwada (Rajaura) Raes of Kandoi (Bulandshahr) was the first Jat Superintendent of Police in the country.

Surjit Kaur Deol Jat was the first woman IPS officer, from the 1956 batch, although it is commonly misattributed to Kiran Bedi.

Pradeep Singh Malik became the first Jat Civil Service topper in the 2019 batch.

Harnaaz Sandhu made history as the first Jat Miss Universe in 2021, while Aishwarya Sheoran was crowned the first Jat Miss India in 2020.

Abhilasa Badak became the first woman combat aviator in India and is a Jat.

Riya Kadwasra was the first woman Jat topper of the Combined Defense Services Examination (CDS) in 2022.

Ms. Harita Kaur Deol Jat is recognized as the first Jat woman Air Force pilot to fly an aircraft solo, accomplishing this feat in 1994 when she flew an AVRO-HS-748 at an altitude of 10,000 feet.

Shanan Dhaka is the topper of first women's National Defence Academy (NDA) examination in the year 2021.

Maharaja Ranjit Singh's victories in the Indian subcontinent were more significant than those of Napoleon Bonaparte in Europe.

Sardar Bhagat Singh and Kartar Singh Sarabha standout as eminent freedom fighters in Indian history. Among the Panj Pyaras (the five beloved ones of Sikh faith) was Jat Dharam Singh Dalal of Hastinapur. Jat Bhai Jaito Ji and Bhai Dullo Ji played crucial roles in retrieving the severed head of Guru Tegh Bahadur Ji,allegedly hung in Chandni Chowk by the orders of Mughal King Aurangzeb, and safely transporting it to Anandpur Sahib through a perilous journey. Notable Jats such as Baba Buddha Ji Randhawa and Baba Bala Ji Sandhu were disciples of Guru Nanak Dev Ji, while Baba Bir Singh Ghuman fell martyr to the Sikh cause during the time of the 6th Guru, Hargobind Ji.

Jats serve as a refuge against the oppression faced by lower castes within Hindu society. They maintain an egalitarian social structure, valuing every individual equally, whether they are a Chief Minister or a farmer tilling their land. Prominent Jat leaders include Chaudhary Baldev Ram Mirdha, Ch. Charan Singh, Ch. Devi Lal, Dr. Bal Ram Jakhar, Ch. Ram Niwas Mirdha and Ch. Kumbha Ram Arya.

Mahendra Chaudhary notably served as the Prime Minister of Fiji from May 19, 1999, to May 27, 2000.

The Jats of Punjab, Haryana, and western Uttar Pradesh were pivotal in the Green Revolution, making India self-sufficient and surplus in food grains. However, they now face distress as their land holdings have diminished due to multiple bifurcations, making agriculture less profitable. It is crucial for the government to address these challenges.

Several sayings reflect Jat culture: (1) "Jat mara tub janiye jub tehrmi ho jaye" – a Jat is only considered dead after the obituary rites are completed on the 13th day after death. (2) "Unpadh Jat padhe brabar aur padha Jat Khuda brabar" –an uneducated Jat is as good as an educated one, and an educated Jat is akin to God. (3) "Jat ganna na de pur bheli de" — a Jat may not give a sugarcane but may offer a lump of jaggery if asked respectfully.

During his tenure (September 1943 - March 1947), Indian Viceroy Lord Wavell expressed to his ADC, Captain Raghubir Singh, the need for a Jat to write their history in English, fearing that outsiders might misrepresent it.

This article aims to illuminate and educate people about the Jats, challenging false stereotypes and generalizations. The intent is not to promote chauvinism or narrow-mindedness but to revive and establish Jat history, which has often been overlooked or obscured by less generous narratives in the broader context of Indian history.

●●●

28

Subtle Characteristics of Jats

The Jats have a rich history, originally living in large tribes across regions straddling the borders of Iran and Afghanistan. Their unique marital customs, which traditionally exclude a few tribes, have contributed to their genetic strength, both mentally and physically, making them less prone to disease over generations. Jats have rich dietary habits with heavy lactose tolerance .Over time, the term "Jat" evolved from a designation of tribe to a caste, while tribal councils transformed into KhapPanchayats.Jat, in fact, is the conglomeration of interconnected multitude of tribes. All tribes are equal in social status. Jats were initially Buddhists and their vegetarian dietary habit still endures. The last Buddhist king was Maharaja Harsh Vardhan Bains when Chinese Buddhist pilgrim Huen Tsang came.

The significance of the word "Jat" extends beyond mere classification; it carries social status and identity. Former Minister of External Affairs, Shri K. Natwar Singh, reportedly noted in his book Maharaja Surajmal that the word itself conveys a sense of pride and belonging. This is reflected in popular culture, including Punjabi films where characters proudly assert their Jat identity. For example, one popular song humorously depicts a Jat advising his wife to only chastise him while he sleeps, illustrating the strong cultural ties and camaraderie within the community.

At its core, being a Jat signifies a commitment to justice and resilience against oppression, regardless of the adversary's power. The British recognized the significance of Jat soldiers, leveraging their might in both World Wars, which underscores the importance of this identity.

It's essential to challenge and dismantle the misconceptions and stereotypes surrounding the Jat community by spreading accurate information. A notable instance from the India- Pakistan War of 1971 illustrates this ethos: Major Hoshiar Singh, A Param Veer Chakra winner, during a critical moment in the Shakargarh sector, reportedly urged his Subedar Major not to vacate the post in case anything untoward happened to him- emphasizing that true Jats do not abandon their posts in times of crisis. This tenacity encapsulates how the identity of being a Jat serves as a guiding force through life's challenges.

29

Why Are Jats Called "16 Duni (Double) 8"?

The term "16 duni (double) 8" is a tribute to the Jats' remarkable resilience and adaptability in the face of adversity. Far from being derogatory, it reflects their innate ability to navigate and overcome challenges, no matter how daunting.

Historically, the Jats settled in the North West of India and faced numerous invasions. For instance, during the rule of Jat King Shashi Ray in Sindh, his reign was reportedly violently usurped by his Brahmin priest, Rai Chach, illustrating the trials they endured.

The invasions of figures like Mohammed Ghazni and Ghori saw the Jats not only resist but also retaliate. Ghazni's final campaign against the Jats in 1027 AD was a direct response to their defiance during his earlier raids. Notably, Jats played a significant role in the assassination of Ghori in 1206 AD and stood firm against the Muslim commanders.

During Tamarlane's invasion in 1398 AD, Jats mobilized their forces but were ultimately outnumbered. Despite suffering reportedly immense losses—over a hundred thousand captured and subjected to atrocities—their indomitable spirit remained unbroken.

In more recent history, during the time of Sir Chhotu Ram, the Jats faced financial hardships under moneylenders. Chhotu Ram's Agricultural Land Alienation Bill helped protect them, a reminder of their enduring struggles. Today, while Jats confront a severe agrarian crisis, their historical resilience persists.

The phrase "16 duni (double) 8" encapsulates the essence of the Jat spirit: hardworking, resourceful, and ever-prepared to defend their dignity and land. Historians recognize that while they toil in fields, they are ever-ready to turn their ploughshares into swords when necessary. Jat Hindus and Jat Sikhs have historically been at the forefront of challenges against oppressive rule, showcasing their charismatic and unwavering survival instincts. This legacy of adaptability and strength continues to define the Jat identity.

●●●

30

The Jats : A Legacy of Resilience and Valor

Once, while perusing a book on the formidable conqueror Tamerlane, authored by a foreign writer, I stumbled upon a remarkable historical account about the Jats. This book, which I borrowed from the American School library in Damascus, Syria, revealed that Jats, known for their martial prowess, had traveled to the Middle East and the Russian republics for military service, often serving as mercenary soldiers. In one such instance, Jat warriors became stranded in Transoxiana, now Uzbekistan, due to geopolitical shifts, unable to return to India. They converted to Islam and rose to power, with their leader bearing the title of "Jat Khan." Tamerlane, the infamous conqueror, initially served as the general under Jat Khan, only to later conspire with his brother-in-law to assassinate him. Though Jat Khan's son sought revenge, his efforts were in vain.

When Tamerlane invaded India in 1398, these Jats saw an opportunity to return to their homeland, but they did not fight for their former general. After passing through a phase of Buddhism, they reconverted to Hinduism. Some historians have erroneously suggested that the Jats are of foreign descent, but in truth, they are indigenous to the subcontinent, with roots dating as far back as the Mahabharata era (circa 3102 BC). They originally resided in the regions straddling Iran and Afghanistan, and later migrated to the Gangetic plain due to changing geopolitical conditions. Over time, their large tribal structures evolved into what is known today as *Khaps*, with their councils transforming into Khap Panchayats. Jats have maintained a unique genetic practice of avoiding marriage within their own or closely related tribes for generations. This tradition of leaving out four tribes in marriage - one's own or the father's, mother's, and both grandmothers' - has fostered a strong sense of tribal unity, and it's believed to have kept the Jats physically and mentally robust.

A Jat is undeniably a true son of the soil. Throughout history, they have been unwavering in their defense of the motherland against foreign aggression, a tradition that continues to this day. Known for their audacity, Jats were renowned for harassing retreating enemy forces, showing little regard for the danger involved. Even in the most perilous times, they continued to till their land with swords girded at their waists, ready to leap into battle at a moment's notice. Their ability to quickly organize against foreign invaders was legendary. As described reportedly by former Foreign Minister Shri K. Natwar Singh in his book *Maharaja Surajmal*, "Jats kept their gaze at the ploughshares , but when the right opportunity came, they turned their ploughshares into swords."

In Russian, the word "Jat" is synonymous with being headstrong, a desperado, or intrepid. The resilience and unique spirit of the Jats are captured in several proverbs and sayings:

- "Jat marya tub janiye jub tehrmi ho jaye" - A Jat should be considered dead only after the 13th day of their demise, reflecting their indomitable spirit and refusal to give up easily.
- "Unpadh Jat padhe brabar aur padha Jat khuda brabar" - An uneducated Jat is as capable as an educated one, and an educated Jat is as powerful as God, underscoring the Jats' natural intelligence and determination.
- "Jat ganna na de pur bheli de" - A Jat may not give a sugarcane, but will offer a lump of jaggery if requested with respect, illustrating their generosity when approached with humility.

The Jats' legacy of resilience, strength, and fearlessness has been etched into history, and their contributions to the defense of India remain unparalleled.

●●●

31

Analysis of "Reforms Should Make Farming Sustainable" by Devinder Sharma

In his article published in The Tribune on January 13, 2022, Devinder Sharma highlights the concerning failure of Indian policymakers to learn from the agricultural market reforms in the United States. Despite the repeal of three contentious farm laws, the prevailing belief persists that "supply and demand equilibrium will lead to price discovery." One must question how long this flawed ideology will endure.

President Joe Biden has acknowledged the plight of livestock farmers in the U.S., noting that while ranchers once received 60 cents of every dollar spent on beef, they now earn only 39 cents. Similarly, hog farmers' share has plummeted from 48-50 cents to a mere 19 cents. This stark decline highlights the significant profits being amassed by large corporations. For instance, the U.S. Department of Agriculture (USDA) reports that beef prices have risen by 21%, pork by 17%, and chicken by 8%, yet the income for farmers continues to plummet.

U.S. Agriculture Secretary Tom Vilsack illustrated this disparity with the story of an Iowa farmer who lost $150 per head while the processor made a profit of $1,800 per head. In India, we often blame commission agents and traders for farmer exploitation, yet we must recognize that four meat processing giants control 85% of the U.S. meat industry. This raises the question: are they not simply the largest middlemen? In India, there is a campaign to discredit commission agents, paving the way for agribusiness companies under the guise of reform.

While regulating middlemen is necessary, we must also reflect on the American experience, where consolidation has devastated livestock farmers. This has resulted in a significant decline in prices, forcing many family-run farms to the brink of financial ruin. The collapse of American farming serves as a testament to the destructive nature of free-market policies in agriculture.

The persistent failure of "supply demand equilibrium" to provide fair prices for farmers, both in the U.S. and globally, reveals a troubling trend of monopolization that exploits both producers and consumers. The U.S. National Farmers Union has launched a campaign for "Fairness to Farmers," advocating for the enforcement of antitrust laws against corporate monopolies.

In response, President Biden has initiated measures to support smaller meat processors, acknowledging the detrimental impact of monopolies on the economy. However, these efforts do not solve the underlying issue. The real solution lies in guaranteeing remunerative prices for agricultural producers. This demand for a "guaranteed price" was notably emphasized during the tractor protests in Washington, D.C., in 1979.

Indian farmers are rightly insisting on a legally sanctioned guaranteed price, ensuring no transactions occur below a specified benchmark. This call for fair compensation is echoed by farmers in Europe as well. The ongoing global farm crisis is rooted in declining farm incomes, exacerbated by a lack of supportive policies.

In Canada, the National Farmers Union has reported that farmer prices in 2005 were lower than during the Great Depression, despite overall economic growth. They advocate for a "Farm Income Support Program" that could address up to 95% of farmers' production costs.

Both the U.S. and Canada have overlooked the legitimate demands for guaranteed prices, reflecting a broader failure in economic policy to recognize the urgent need for a "living income" for farmers.

Ultimately, farmers worldwide are shouldering the burden of producing food at a loss. Therefore, India must resist handing farmers over to corporate interests. Instead, we should enact laws that guarantee Minimum Support Prices (MSP) with legal enforcement, demonstrating a commitment to uplifting farmers from poverty and preventing the tragic cycle of indebtedness and suicide.

●●●

32

Need for Course Correction in Indian History

In 1957, Marshal Zhukov, a legendary commander of the former Soviet army, addressed Indian cadets at the Indian Military Academy in Dehradun. During his speech, he asserted that Alexander the Great never defeated King Porus (Pururava) in the renowned Battle of the Hydaspes (located at the Jhelum River in Punjab) in May 326 BC, a misconception that has been perpetuated by European narratives.

While traveling abroad, I attended a cultural event organized by the Jat Association in the USA, where an elderly American recounted an interesting piece of history. He noted that prior to engaging in battle with King Porus, Alexander sent his Macedonian vanguards to scout the area. These troops approached menacingly, attempting to intimidate the local populace as they sought passage through ripe wheat fields. However, the Indian farmers, predominantly from the Jat Dahiya and Kang tribes, refused to let them cross their fields and instead directed them through hilly areas.

Determined to resist, these farmers—who were also skilled soldiers—formed small detachments and ambushed the Macedonian scouts, systematically defeating them. The audacity of the Jat soldiers extended even to attacking Alexander's military camp. Upon learning of this, Alexander was furious and devised a treacherous plan to besiege the Jat villages through pincer attacks. Unfortunately, during this assault, the villages were left vulnerable, as all able-bodied men had gone off to battle. The old, women, and children were taken captive.

In a desperate move, Alexander sent a message to the leader of the Jat farmers, demanding their surrender without a fight. He threatened that if they resisted, he would execute one hundred hostages daily. Faced with this impossible choice, the leader called upon five trusted confidantes and instructed them to bring him fresh wheat on a large saucer. He then asked them to behead him and place his severed head on the wheat, covering it with a cloth. They were to deliver this grim message to Alexander, proclaiming that he had sacrificed himself to prevent the genocide of innocent people, as Alexander's true fight was against him, not the innocents.

It is said that upon receiving the severed head of the Jat leader, Alexander wept, a rare display of emotion—reportedly the only two times he cried in his life were for the Jat leader and later for his beloved horse during the conflict against the Jats. To secure the release of the hostages, Alexander demanded that the Jat farmers replenish his ranks with soldiers, effectively blackmailing them into fighting against their own kin. This episode illustrates that Alexander did not truly defeat King Porus, underscoring and reinforcing the urgent need to rectify the portrayal of such events in Indian history.

The prevailing narrative that Indians fell like ninepins before invading forces is not only misleading but undermines the valor and resilience of the Jat community, a proud and significant part of our nation's heritage. It is crucial to amend these historical inaccuracies to honor the true legacy of resistance and strength that characterized our ancestors.

●●●

33

Review of "A Survey of Indian History" by K. M. Panikkar

K.M. Panikkar's "A Survey of Indian History" stands as a significant scholarly contribution to the understanding of India's complex past. Panikkar, with his impressive credentials—including his education at Oxford and extensive diplomatic career—brings a unique perspective to the narrative of Indian history.

The book is structured into three main parts: Ancient Indian history, Medieval Indian history and Modern Indian history. Panikkar's approach to categorizing these periods is useful, yet he acknowledges the shortcomings in traditional historical accounts, particularly their tendency to focus on dynasties and kings rather than the broader tapestry of civilization.

One of the book's notable strengths is its examination of the socio-political landscape of ancient and medieval India. However, the author occasionally overlooks significant details that could enhance the narrative. For instance, while Panikkar discusses the impact of invaders like Mahmud Ghazni and Muhammad Ghori, he could have expanded on the resistance efforts of groups like the Jats, whose contributions to Indian history are often marginalized.

In his exploration of the first Battle of Tarain in 1191 AD in which Prithviraj Chauhan won and Second Battle of Tarain in 1192 AD in which Mohammad Ghori won and the subsequent resistance led by the Jats, Panikkar highlights a critical aspect of Indian history that deserves more attention. The omission of details regarding the Jats' mobilization and their significant role in various historical events—such as the resistance against Qutubudin Aibek and Allaudin Khilji—reveals a gap that future editions might address.

Panikkar's commentary on figures like Rezia Begum and the political dynamics of her reign reflects a nuanced understanding of gender and power in Indian history. However, more contextual information about the Jats' support for her would provide a richer narrative.

The author's reflections on the socio-economic conditions during the Delhi Sultanate and the Mughals are insightful, yet he sometimes overlooks the grassroots movements and uprisings that challenged imperial authority, particularly those led by the Jats. The mention of Maharaja Surajmal and his diplomatic strategies against invaders like Ahmed Shah Abdali, while commendable, also highlights the need for a more thorough examination of Jat resistance.

While Panikkar asserts that foreign invaders ruled India as Indians, this assertion merits deeper exploration, particularly concerning the cultural assimilation and local governance strategies employed by various rulers. His assertion regarding Aurangzeb's commitment to Indian unity is a provocative claim that invites further discussion and analysis.

Overall, "A Survey of Indian History" is a robust work, albeit with some gaps in its exploration of certain groups and events. Panikkar's scholarship is commendable, and his insights into the socio-political fabric of India are invaluable. Future revisions could benefit from a more inclusive examination of the diverse forces that have shaped Indian history, particularly the contributions and resistances of communities like the Jats. Despite its omissions, this book remains an essential read for anyone seeking a deeper understanding of India's historical narrative.

●●●

34

Review of the book- India After Gandhi, A History by Ramachandra Guha.

Over the past few days, I have read the comprehensive book India After Gandhi: A History by the renowned author Ramachandra Guha. The book bears some similarities to the NCERT history textbook (Part III) taught in Indian schools at the 12th-grade level, but it introduces a few new revelations along with some notable omissions. In Part Three, titled "Shaking the Centre," the book reflects on key historical moments, such as the years 1757 and 1857, which are deeply ingrained in Indian history. However, the crucial fact that Haryana existed as a large region, comprising present-day Haryana, western UP, and parts of Rajasthan before 1858, has been overlooked. Notably, the people of Haryana, along with its Rajas and Zamindars, participated fiercely in the 1857 revolt, so much so that Haryana was disbanded as a state on February 6, 1858, as punishment. It is often mistakenly believed that Haryana only came into existence on

November 1, 1966, following its bifurcation from Punjab.

On pages 171, 211, and 221, the book mentions the Bhakra Dam project, which was completed after India gained independence. However, it fails to note that the project was actually approved on January 8, 1945, just one day before Sir Chhotu Ram's death on January 9, 1945. On page 11, under the heading "Picking Up the Pieces," Guha writes: "At the end of 1946, one province that had escaped the rioting was Punjab. In office were the Unionists, a coalition of Muslim, Hindu, and Sikh landlords. They held the peace uncertainly, for ranged against them were the militant Muslim Leaguers on the one side and the no less militant Sikh political party, the Akali Dal, on the other." What is conspicuously missing here is the role of Sir Chhotu Ram, who united farmers of different faiths—Hindu, Muslim, and Sikh—by aligning their economic interests. He co-founded the Unionist Party in 1923 alongside Sir Fazal Hussain. Even though Sir Chhotu Ram passed away in 1945, 81 Muslim MLAs remained in the Unionist Party, with even the two lone Muslim League MLAs aligned with it. Sir Chhotu Ram was such a powerful figure that, on March 10, 1944, he had Mohammad Ali Jinnah ousted from Punjab within 24 hours under the orders of Premier Khizar Hayat Tiwana. Notably, Jinnah's ouster did not spark any protests in his favor. Many believe that had Sir Chhotu Ram not passed away in 1945, he could have potentially averted the tragic Partition of the subcontinent along religious lines.

The book contains a new revelation that George Orwell initially called Mahatma Gandhi a "humbug," but later came to regard him as a saint. It also notes that

VP Menon, who played a key role in the integration of princely states, rose from the ranks of a clerk to an important position in the administration. At the time of India's independence, there were 565 princely states, and the rulers were given the option of joining either India or Pakistan. Maharaja Ganga Singh of Bikaner was the first to sign on with the Indian Union. However, the book omits the fact that Ch. Devi Lal was unanimously declared Prime Minister-elect on December 1, 1989, though he ultimately passed the position to VP Singh and became the Deputy Prime Minister. Similarly, there is no mention of Dr. Balram Jakhar, who served two terms as Lok Sabha Speaker—the longest tenure of any Speaker in India's history—and later became the Agriculture Minister under the PV Narasimha Rao government. The absence of Chaudhary Charan Singh, who served as Prime Minister of India, is also glaring.

On page 657, the book mentions the contribution of the Naga Regiment, which was well-suited to the cold environment and played a pivotal role in the Kargil Conflict. However, it is perplexing and somewhat misleading that the Jats have been completely ignored. Of the reportedly 471 casualties in the Kargil Conflict, 322 were Jats from across India, with 171 of them hailing from Haryana alone.

The book also recounts how the Maharaja of Jodhpur was given a blank signed letterhead by Mohammad Ali Jinnah, allowing him to add any conditions he wished in order to merge with Pakistan. This plan was swiftly foiled by KM Pannikar, the Dewan of Bikaner state, who informed the government. This event dealt a blow to Jinnah's 'Two-Nation Theory,' as Jodhpur, a Hindu-majority state ruled by a Hindu Maharaja, chose not to join Pakistan.

After independence, relations between Jawaharlal Nehru and Sardar Patel were strained. Nehru favored C. Rajagopalachari for the presidency of India, but Patel supported Dr. Rajendra Prasad, who eventually became the country's first President. Similarly, Nehru wanted Rajagopalachari to lead the Congress Party, but Patel backed Purushottam Das Tandon, who was ultimately elected as Congress President.

Finally, during the midnight swearing-in ceremony on August 15, 1947, Nehru was administered the oath as Prime Minister. There was a minor mishap, however, as the envelope given to Lord Mountbatten, which was supposed to contain the names of the ministers to be sworn in alongside Nehru, was found to be empty. Fortunately, this error was quickly rectified, and the proper list was provided to Mountbatten, allowing the ceremony to proceed smoothly.

●●●

35

Chaudhary Devi Lal : The Kingmaker

Chaudhary Devi Lal was undoubtedly one of the most remarkable leaders India has ever produced. He became the Chief Minister of Haryana in 1978 and subsequently in 1987, and from that point onward, his influence rapidly expanded to Delhi and beyond, making his name resonate from Gujarat to Bihar and the southern regions of the country. His popularity soared, and slogans such as "Tau poora tolega, aur Lal Qile se bolega"—translated as "Tau (Chaudhary Devi Lal) will deliver fully and will address the nation from the ramparts of the Red Fort"—became commonplace, hinting at his ambition to become Prime Minister.

A massive farmers' rally held at Boat Club in Delhi on September 25, 1989, to celebrate his birthday attracted an estimated 500,000 attendees. The release of white pigeons during the event, with two perched on his green turban, was seen as an auspicious sign. Chaudhary Devi Lal reached the pinnacle of his political career when he was unanimously elected Prime Minister of India on December 1, 1989, a position he ultimately chose to transfer to Shri V.P. Singh, a decision that remains a subject of speculation among historians and political analysts.

His popularity stemmed from his deep understanding of rural life. He spoke the language of the villagers, using familiar aphorisms, humor, and idioms that endeared him to them. During his election campaigns, he promised to initiate an old-age pension scheme, which was initially ridiculed by his opponents as impractical. In a characteristic rural manner, he vowed that his secretary would bring him the file with notings authorizing the pension and loan waivers on which he would append his signatures , a promise that resonated with the people and led to a landslide victory, with 85 seats won out of 90 in Haryana.

Chaudhary Devi Lal's ancestors migrated from the princely state of Bikaner to present-day Haryana. His great-grandfather, Chaudhary Teja Ram, was an enterprising landowner who purchased 3,000 acres in Haryana, leading to the establishment of the village named "Teja Khera" in his honor. Chaudhary Devi Lal was born on September 25, 1914, to Chaudhary Lekh Ram and Smt. Sugna Devi. His father was a follower of Mahatma Gandhi and was imprisoned for two years for participating in the Quit India Movement. Originally named Devi Dayal, Chaudhary Devi Lal received an education up to the middle standard and was an accomplished wrestler in an Akhara in Badal village, Punjab. He abandoned his studies to join the freedom movement alongside his brother, Chaudhary Sahib Ram, and endured rigorous imprisonment, spending time in Hissar jail.

Married to Smt. Harki Devi, he had four sons: Chaudhary Om Prakash Chautala, Chaudhary Pratap Singh, Chaudhary Ranjit Singh, and Chaudhary Jagdish. He participated in the freedom struggle in 1932 and was recognized as a delegate of the All India Congress Committee in 1938. During that time, his brother was elected MLA, further solidifying their political legacy.

Chaudhary Devi Lal could not contest in the provincial assembly election in 1937 from Punjab because he was under age hence his elder brother Chaudhary Sahib Ram contested the election. Chaudhary Devi Lal and his brother had declared that their party would abolish the Zamindari system from the Punjab, which annoyed the big landlords and their henchmen. One day when Chaudhary Devi Lal was addressing an election rally then three assailants fired at him but he ducked the fire but his alert bodyguard- a handsome Bishnoi Jat youth killed all the three assailants on the spot. When this bodyguard was brought before the British Judge then the Judge recorded in the case file, " He is too handsome to be hanged". The bodyguard was declared scot free. It is for record that the bodyguard was the most handsome youth in the area.

Chaudhary Devi Lal was a staunch opponent of the feudal and Zamindari systems. After India gained independence, he initiated a farmers' movement that resulted in his arrest along with 500 supporters. This led to an amendment of the tenant act, ensuring fair treatment for tenants. Despite his feudal background, he advocated for land ownership by those who tilled it, even giving much of his own land to tenants. His efforts contributed to the abolition of the Zamindari system in Punjab, an achievement that paralleled Sir Chhotu Ram's passing of the Agriculture Land Alienation Bill during British rule, protecting farmers from exploitation by moneylenders.

Elected to the Punjab Assembly in 1952 and serving as the Congress President of Punjab in 1956, he faced political challenges when Haryana was formed in 1966. Ignoring his claims for leadership, the government appointed Pandit Bhagat Dayal Sharma as Chief Minister. Chaudhary Devi Lal subsequently played a pivotal role in toppling Sharma's government, allowing Rao Birender Singh and Chaudhary Bansi Lal to ascend, thus establishing himself as a kingmaker in state politics.

In 1971, he left the Congress Party after nearly four decades and won a by-election in 1974. Following the declaration of Emergency by Smt. Indira Gandhi in 1975, he, along with other opposition leaders, was imprisoned for 19 months. When the Emergency was lifted, he was elected Chief Minister of Haryana, earning the title "Sher-e-Haryana" (Lion of Haryana) for his staunch opposition to dictatorial rule.

From 1980 to 1982, he served as a Member of Parliament. His party, Lok Dal, formed a coalition with the BJP, becoming the largest party in the Haryana Assembly elections of 1982. However, despite being asked by Governor G.D. Tapase to prove his majority, the government installed Chaudhary Bhajan Lal as Chief Minister, a move criticized as a blow to democracy.

Chaudhary Devi Lal launched the "NayayaYudh" (War for Justice) campaign, leading to a remarkable victory in the 1987 Haryana Assembly elections, securing 85 out of 90 seats. He served as Chief Minister for a second term, appointing Dr. K.V. Singh as his Officer on Special Duty. Though he was unanimously elected Prime Minister on December 1, 1989, he transferred this honor to V.P. Singh, a decision that remains enigmatic. He later became Deputy Prime Minister and Agriculture Minister but was expelled from the government in July 1990 due to political disagreements with V.P. Singh.

The fallout from the halt of L.K. Advani's rath yatra led the BJP to withdraw its support, resulting in a loss of parliamentary majority. Chaudhary Devi Lal once again emerged as a kingmaker, facilitating Chandra Sekhar's rise to the Prime Ministership with Congress support. However, this alliance was short-lived, ending abruptly when Rajiv Gandhi withdrew support over alleged allegations of espionage.

Elected to the Rajya Sabha in 1998, Chaudhary Devi Lal passed away on April 6, 2001. Known as the "Tau" of the nation, he was a fervent advocate for the rights of farmers and the underprivileged. His enduring legacy as a towering figure in rural India is solidified by his demand for reserving half of all governor positions for rural candidates.

●●●

36

Dr. Balram Jakhar : A Fine Combination of Brain and Brawn

Dr. Balram Jakhar stands out as one of India's greatest leaders, possessing a unique blend of warmth, sophistication, and charisma. Standing at 6 feet 5 inches, his magnetic personality allowed him to connect effortlessly with everyone, from humble farmers to esteemed intellectuals. As the longest-serving Speaker of the Lok Sabha, he was not only highly erudite but also a bibliophile and a learned individual, often referred to as a gentle colossus. Dr. Jakhar graduated from Forman Christian College in Lahore in 1945 and was a polyglot, fluent in English, Sanskrit, Hindi, Urdu, and Punjabi.

Born on August 23, 1923, to Chaudhary Rajaram Jakhar and Smt. Patodevi in Panchkosi village, Fazilka district (now Abohar, Punjab), Dr. Jakhar started his family business in farming, modernizing techniques for developing orchards and vineyards. His contributions to fruit growing earned him national recognition in

1975, culminating in the prestigious title of "All India Udyan Pandit," awarded by the President of India. His leadership within the farming community propelled him into national politics. He was elected to the Punjab Legislative Assembly in 1972 and, just a year later, appointed Deputy Minister of Cooperatives, Irrigation, and Power, serving in that capacity until 1977.

Despite the Congress Party's setbacks in 1977, Dr. Jakhar won re-election and became the leader of the opposition in the Punjab Legislative Assembly from 1977 to 1980. He entered the Lok Sabha in 1980 from the Ferozepur constituency and was elected Speaker of the Lok Sabha on January 22, 1980. Although he had no prior experience as a presiding officer, Dr. Jakhar handled the role with remarkable confidence, innate common sense, and an understanding that the House should govern its own procedures in a parliamentary democracy.

Re-elected to the 8th Lok Sabha from Sikar in Rajasthan in 1984, Dr. Jakhar again served as Speaker, earning the distinction of being the only Speaker to chair two consecutive Lok Sabhas for their full terms. He initiated significant reforms in parliamentary procedures, including the automation and computerization of parliamentary work. His efforts greatly enhanced the Parliament library and improved the reference, research, and documentation systems. He was also instrumental in establishing the Parliament Museum and Archives, highlighting his commitment to innovation.

Under his leadership, the review of the Rules of Procedure and Conduct of Business in the Lok Sabha was undertaken for the first time since 1952, introducing judicious updates to the rules. He oversaw the landmark "Anti-Defection Legislation of 1985" and provided courageous interpretations of the roles and limitations of the judiciary in relation to Parliament, advocating that the government must operate within the boundaries set by the Constitution of India. Notably, the Standing Committee System was introduced during the 10th Lok Sabha under his guidance, following extensive deliberations.

Dr. Jakhar firmly ruled that the courts could not compel Speakers to appear in defense of their decisions related to parliamentary functioning. He made history as the first Asian elected Chairman of the Commonwealth Parliamentary Executive Forums. In 1991, he served as Agriculture Minister under Prime Minister P.V. Narasimha Rao. He later held the position of Governor of Madhya Pradesh from June 30, 2004, to May 30, 2009, where he played a pivotal role in enhancing the welfare of farmers through scientific techniques.

Throughout his career, Dr. Jakhar was a four-time Member of Parliament, having been elected in 1980, 1984, 1991, and 1998. He chaired various committees, including the Business Advisory Committee, Rules Committee, General Purpose Committee, and the Standing Committee of the Conference of Presiding Officers of Legislative Bodies of India. Additionally, he was a life member of Bharat Krishak Samaj and served as President of the Jallianwala Bagh Memorial Trust Management Committee. He authored the insightful book *People, Parliament and Administration* and led a farmers' delegation to the International Agricultural Producers Conference in Washington, D.C.

A prominent figure in Punjab's agricultural sector, Dr. Jakhar served as President of the Punjab Cooperative Grape Growers Federation and the Farmers Forum of Punjab. In recognition of his contributions to agriculture and horticulture, Haryana Agricultural University honored him with an honorary degree of Doctor of Science. He also received the honorary title of "Vidya Martand" from Gurukul Kangadi Vishwavidyalaya in Haridwar, Uttar Pradesh.

Dr. Jakhar had diverse interests, including sports, farming, and reading. He was a multi-talented individual, proficient in Sanskrit, Hindi, and English. Unfortunately, he passed away on February 3, 2016, after a brief illness. His invaluable contributions to public life will always be remembered, and he will be celebrated as a popular leader who enriched India's parliamentary democracy throughout his long political career, emerging as a flamboyant Speaker of the Lok Sabha for two consecutive terms.

●●●

37

Dr. Sarup Singh : A Legend in His Lifetime

Dr. Sarup Singh was a distinguished educationist and an intellectual of international acclaim, rising from humble beginnings to remarkable heights. Known for his unwavering work ethic and integrity, he was a visionary who generously guided his students and held firm convictions throughout his life. Originating from the obscure village of Sanghi in Rohtak district, Haryana, he exemplified high professional standards and achieved the pinnacle of his career when he was appointed Vice Chancellor of the prestigious Delhi University in the heart of India's national capital, becoming a living legend in his lifetime.

A poignant story, though possibly apocryphal, underscores his humble beginnings. Upon returning to Sanghi after earning his PhD in English, villagers celebrated him as "Doctor." An innocent farmer approached him for medical help for his sick son. Dr. Sarup Singh clarified that he was not a medical doctor, prompting the farmer to return later with an ailing buffalo, only to be met with the same response. Frustrated, the farmer exclaimed, "If you are not a doctor of humans or animals, what kind of doctor are you?" This tale highlights the immense challenges Dr. Sarup Singh faced in his journey to success amid the difficult circumstances of his village.

Born on January 9, 1917, in Sanghi, Dr. Sarup Singh received his early education locally before transferring to Jat High School in Rohtak. He later moved to Delhi to pursue higher education at Delhi University. Endowed with exceptional communication skills, he caught the attention of his teacher, Shri B.B. Gupta, who recognized his potential while grading his examination papers. Shri Gupta mentored him, offering advice on personality development, which helped refine Dr. Sarup Singh both internally and externally. He excelled academically, topping his BA Honors in English in 1938 and achieving first division in his M.A. English in 1940, despite the personal tragedy of losing his wife on the day of his final exam.

Dr. Sarup Singh began his career as a tutor for undergraduate classes at Hindu College in Delhi, eventually becoming a regular lecturer and warden of a hostel, where he demonstrated remarkable administrative skills. He later married again, and he and his wife warmly hosted visitors from their village. He had two sons from his first marriage and two daughters from his second.

He was invited to serve as Vice Principal at Jat College in Rohtak with a promise of future promotion to Principal.

However, disillusioned with the college atmosphere, he returned to Hindu College as a lecturer in English. Under the guidance of Shri B.B. Gupta, who continued to mentor him, Dr. Sarup Singh pursued his doctorate at the University of London, overcoming financial struggles and completing his studies in just two years. His thesis gained recognition when it was published in the *Times Literary Supplement*, a notable achievement.

Dr. Sarup Singh was invited by Shri Hardwari Lal, Principal of Kirorimal College, to join as Vice Principal. Under his leadership, the college flourished. His brilliance led to close collaboration with the Vice Chancellor of Delhi University, Shri C.D. Deshmukh, who often sought his advice on university matters. Dr. Sarup Singh eventually became a Professor and Head of the English Department at Delhi University.

Famous economist Shri K.N. Raj accepted the Vice Chancellor position at Delhi University on the condition that Dr. Sarup Singh would serve as Pro-Vice Chancellor alongside him. Following Shri Raj's departure, Dr. Sarup Singh was appointed acting Vice Chancellor. He adeptly managed the sensitive Salman College incident, where a teacher from a minority community married a Hindu girl, triggering protests. His handling of this situation made him indispensable to Delhi University, and he was formally appointed Vice Chancellor in 1971, becoming the first Delhi University alumnus to hold this position.

During his tenure, he implemented significant innovations, including the establishment of the South Delhi campus, merging the PG Institute of Evening

Studies with relevant departments, launching a non-college women's delegation, and founding a Medical Science College. He oversaw the construction of an Administrative Block and staff quarters (Sarup Nagar), and recognized both the Karamchari Union and the Delhi University Students Union. His rapport with the Vice President of India, who served as Chancellor of Delhi University, was noteworthy; he charmed the Vice President with his approachable demeanor.

Dr. Sarup Singh also met with then-Prime Minister Smt. Indira Gandhi to advocate for political neutrality within Delhi University. While she initially agreed, her later contradictory statements left him disillusioned, leading him to accept a position at a foreign university. Upon returning to India, he became a member of the UPSC, where he argued for equitable treatment of candidates from rural backgrounds during viva voce exams. Later, he was elected as a Member of Parliament from the Rajya Sabha, though he could achieve little from the opposition benches. Known for his wit and humor, he contested the Lok Sabha elections in 1984 from the Rohtak constituency but lost amid the Congress wave.

Dr. Sarup Singh served as Governor of Kerala from 1989 to 1990 before being transferred to Gujarat, where he served until 1995. He achieved a significant milestone by uniting both Leftist and Congress parties during his tenure in Kerala. In 1995, the Delhi government honored him as Distinguished Citizen of Delhi at Talkatora Stadium. He received an honorary D.Litt. from Delhi University in a special convocation in 1998, alongside notable figures such as Nobel laureate Professor Amartya Sen and industrialist Raunaq Singh. He was also a visiting professor at universities in Canberra (Australia), Illinois (USA), and Southern California (USA).

Despite suffering from an abdominal ailment that required surgery at Apollo Hospital in Delhi, he lived for six more years before passing away on August 3, 2003. Dr. Sarup Singh's profound contributions to education and his legacy will be remembered for generations to come.

●●●

38

Kisan Kesari Baldev Ram Mirdha

Chaudhary Baldev Ram Mirdha, known as "Kisan Kesari," was a remarkable leader of farmers from Rajasthan, who fought for the rights of oppressed farmers in the Marwar region. Born on January 17, 1889, in Kuchera village, Nagaur, he came from a humble background, with his father, Chaudhary Mangla Ram, serving in the Department of Posts and Telegraphs. After completing his education, Mirdha joined the police force, where he earned recognition for his role in eliminating notorious dacoits. He rose to the rank of Deputy Inspector General of Police in 1943.

In 1947, Mirdha resigned from government service to dedicate himself to improving the lives of farmers, who were suffering under the oppressive Jagirdari and Zamindari systems. He founded the Marwar Kisan Sabha and later the Rajasthan Kisan Sabha, leading efforts to end feudal exploitation. A notable moment came in 1943, when Mirdha, alongside Sir Chhotu Ram, organized a massive farmers' conference in Jodhpur, attended by the Maharaja of Jodhpur, which boosted the morale and dignity of the oppressed farmers.

Mirdha's political and social reforms significantly impacted Rajasthan. He passed the Tenant Protection Law in 1949, the Rajasthan Land Revenue Law in 1951, and the Land Reform and Resumption of Jagirdars Act in 1952, all of which led to the eventual abolition of the Zamindari system. Despite facing violent resistance from the Zamindars, Mirdha remained fearless and unwavering in his commitment to farmers' welfare.

In addition to his legislative achievements, he established hostels for poor farmers children and worked tirelessly to promote social reforms, advocating against dowry, child marriage, and drinking. He won the first Lok Sabha election from Deguna in 1952.

Chaudhary Baldev Ram Mirdha passed away on August 2, 1953, while en route to address a farmers' conference. His legacy continues through his descendants, including his son Chaudhary Ram Niwas Mirdha, grandson Chaudhary Harendra Mirdha, and great-grandson Raguvendra Mirdha, who all became influential figures in Rajasthan politics.

●●●

39

Dr. Ram Dhan Singh : A Forgotten Hero of Indian Agriculture

Dr. Ram Dhan Singh was a world-renowned agricultural scientist from the Indian subcontinent, whose visionary contributions to agriculture have had a lasting impact. Despite his monumental achievements, it is unfortunate that his work remains underappreciated, particularly at the national level. He is a forgotten hero who deserves recognition, such as the Bharat Ratna, for his contributions. Shockingly, in a city like Delhi, known as the agricultural capital of India, there is no road or institution named after him. His foundational research paved the way for the Green Revolution, a movement widely credited to figures like M.S. Swaminathan, but it was Dr. Singh's groundwork that made it possible.

Born on May 1, 1891, in Kaloi village, Rohtak district (now in Haryana), Dr. Singh came from a family deeply rooted in rural traditions. His father, Chaudhary Shankar Singh Hooda, was a respected landowner, which afforded

Ram Dhan Singh a strong educational foundation. He completed his early education in his village, moving on to pass his Middle School in 1905 and High School in 1907 from Government High School, Rohtak. After earning his Intermediate degree from DAV College, Lahore, in 1909, Dr. Singh pursued a three-year diploma in agriculture at Punjab Agricultural and Research College, Lyallpur (now in Pakistan), where he topped his class in 1912.

His determination for fair pay delayed his entry into service until 1914, when he joined the Imperial Agricultural and Research Institute at Pusa, Bihar. Dr. Singh later pursued further studies at Cambridge University, where he earned an M.A. in Natural Science and a diploma in agriculture in 1922.

Upon his return, he joined the Punjab government in 1925 as a fodder specialist and later became a cereal specialist. From 1926 to 1947, he served as Principal of the Government Agricultural College, Lyallpur. For his contributions to agricultural research, the British government honored him with the title of "Rao Bahadur." After India's Independence, he settled in Sonipat, where he continued his research. His work garnered international recognition, and in 1961, Pakistan awarded him a gold medal for his contributions to agriculture. Remarkably, when he visited Pakistan, President Ayub Khan personally received him at the border. Dr. Singh was also awarded the Roll of Honour by Punjab Agricultural University in 1964.

Among his many achievements, Dr. Singh developed

high-yielding varieties of wheat, such as C-518, C-591, and C-250, as well as Basmati rice varieties like Basmati 370 and Jhona 349. His extensive research into cereal and horticultural crops laid the foundation for increased agricultural productivity across the subcontinent. Indian farmers owe a great debt to his pioneering work. In recognition of his immense contributions, Haryana Agricultural University conferred upon him the degree of Doctor of Science (Honoris Causa).

Despite his far-reaching influence, Dr. Ram Dhan Singh passed away on April 17, 1977, as an unsung hero. His name may not be widely remembered, but his contributions to Indian agriculture remain invaluable. The nation owes a great deal to this forgotten titan of agricultural science.

●●●

40

Chaudhary Charan Singh : The Farmers' Champion and a Misunderstood Giant

A defining moment for the farmers of India came when Chaudhary Charan Singh took the helm of the country's affairs, striving to improve their lives. Chaudhary Charan Singh remains one of the greatest leaders India has ever produced. Born into the humble home of a poor farmer, he rose through sheer perseverance to the pinnacle of power, becoming the 5th Prime Minister of India, serving from July 28, 1979, to January 14, 1980. He is fondly remembered as a champion of India's hardworking farmers.

Chaudhary Charan Singh famously said, "The prosperity of the country passes through its agricultural fields and barns," underscoring his belief in the centrality of agriculture to India's future. Even today, this remains true, with agriculture and allied activities employing over 50% of India's population. Charan Singh had a deep understanding of rural life, speaking the same language, sharing the wit and humor of villagers, and resonating with the poor and disadvantaged. Although he never studied at the London School of Economics, he possessed an innate and realistic knowledge of India's economy. His book, *India: Its Poverty and Its Solution*, is taught at Harvard University, highlighting his expertise in addressing the nation's economic challenges. Charan Singh was a strong advocate for the Gandhian approach to alleviating poverty and unemployment, yet, tragically, he remains one of the most misunderstood giants of Indian politics.

A man of integrity, Charan Singh stood for moral values, transparency, and honesty in public life. He was firmly against caste and religious discrimination, exemplified by the fact that his cook in 1932 was a Dalit, a rare and bold move in those times. He lived simply, epitomizing the principle of "simple living, high thinking." Charan Singh recognized the struggles of small farmers, emphasizing that eight out of every ten farmers barely survived and were perpetually in financial distress. He played a pivotal role in the Green Revolution, which transformed India from a food-deficit country to a food-surplus nation. This success was due to the efforts of leaders like Chaudhary Charan Singh, Chaudhary Devi Lal, and Mahendra Singh Tikait, who fought tirelessly for the rights of farmers.

Despite his contributions, the nation has failed to fully honor Chaudhary Charan Singh's legacy. While Delhi boasts streets named after international figures like Lawrence, Tolstoy, and Canning, there is no road dedicated to this son of the soil. It is not too late to right this wrong.

Charan Singh's honesty in public life was exemplary; he had, proverbially, no skeletons in his cupboard, nor even a door to his cupboard, allowing anyone to look inside. His practical solutions for improving the conditions of the poor included advocating for small-scale industries. Influenced by Mahatma Gandhi and Swami Dayanand, he worked tirelessly to protect the interests of exploited farmers and labourers . Charan Singh often pointed out the inherent injustice faced by farmers, saying, "When a farmer goes to sell his produce, someone else decides the price, and when he goes to buy goods, someone else again sets the price." This captures the core of the exploitation that continues to plague Indian farmers.

Born on September 23, 1902, in Nurpur village, Meerut district, UP, to Chaudhary Mir Singh Tewatia and Netra Kaur, Charan Singh's family had migrated from Ballabgarh after the failed First War of Independence in 1857. Charan Singh graduated with a B.Sc. from Agra College in 1923 and married Gayatri Devi in 1925. He earned a law degree from Agra College and began his legal career in Ghaziabad. Influenced by Mahatma Gandhi, he founded the Congress Committee in Ghaziabad in 1929 and participated in the Civil Disobedience Movement of 1930. His act of making salt illegally from the Hindon River led to six months of imprisonment. In 1942, he led a revolutionary group, resulting in a "shoot at sight" order against him. Charan Singh was eventually arrested and imprisoned for 18 months, during which time he wrote a book on etiquette, *Sistachar*.

After Independence, Charan Singh clashed with Prime Minister Jawaharlal Nehru's vision of cooperative farming, modeled after the USSR's mechanized agriculture. While most Congress leaders hailed Nehru's proposal, Charan Singh vociferously opposed it, preventing what could have been a tragedy for the nation's farmers. His steadfast opposition eventually led to the shelving of the cooperative farming scheme.

As the Agriculture Minister in Dr. Sampurnanand's government in 1952-53, Charan Singh was instrumental in abolishing the oppressive Zamindari system in Uttar Pradesh. His disillusionment with the Congress Party's anti-farmer policies led him to resign and form the Bharatiya Kranti Dal in 1968, pioneering the concept of coalition governments. He served as Chief Minister of UP in 1967 and 1970, and later founded the Lok Dal in 1974, winning 104 seats in the UP Vidhan Sabha and becoming Leader of the Opposition. During the Emergency of 1975, Charan Singh was jailed, along with other opposition leaders.

He played a key role in the formation of the Janata Party in 1977, which eventually came to power. Although he had greater popular support than Morarji Desai, political machinations prevented him from becoming Prime Minister initially. However, on July 28, 1979, he finally assumed the office of Prime Minister, a position he held until January 14, 1980. His principled stance led to his refusal to withdraw cases against Indira Gandhi and her associates for Emergency excesses, resulting in the fall of his government.

Chaudhary Charan Singh passed away on May 25, 1987, and was cremated at Kisan Ghat in Delhi, thanks to the efforts of farmer leaders Chaudhary Mahendra Singh Tikait and Chaudhary Devi Lal. He will forever be remembered as India's first "Kisan Prime Minister," a leader who tirelessly worked for the rights and dignity of the nation's farmers. His legacy continues to inspire, and the nation owes a debt of gratitude to this towering figure who fought for the most marginalized sections of society.

●●●

41

Comments on the Editorial in the Tribune News paper titled "End of Farm protests" dated 11/12/2021.

The paragraph at the fag end of the editorial states that " Projecting MSP as the sole saviour is unrealistic. Tough challenges such as moving away from paddy crop, considering the huge ecological costs that accrue for water- starved Punjab, need to be tackled head- on."

Farmers of the country face an anathema- when a farmer goes to the market to sell his produce, the rates are decided by somebody else. When he goes to the market to buy finished goods, the rates are decided again by somebody else. This is the crux of the exploitation of the farmers of the country. Farmers do not get remunerative prices of their produce. As a result of this farmers accrue loans from the government and private money lenders. When they are not able to pay back the loans, they commit suicides. To provide an example, between 1997 and 2010, 2,50,000 farmers committed suicides in the country.

This calls for creating a price shield or bench mark, below which farmers of the country should not be forced to sell their produce. Farmers want a mechanism through which they should get remunerative prices. This is what MSP is all about. The BJP government had mentioned in its election manifesto during the 2014 general election that they would implement the Swaminathan Commission report which contains the provision of MSP which means total cost + 50% profit on it or C2 +50% profit on it.

70% of our population derives its livelihood from agriculture and its allied activities. To safeguard their livelihood, a minimum support price is absolutely necessary. Insufficient farm income breeds poverty in the villages and the country at large. Rise in rural income will put a brake on unplanned exodus to cities from rural areas, overburdening the civic, housing and health care system. Ever burgeoning ghettos and slums in cities due to mass migration of people from rural areas, is a blot on our country. According to recent World Inequality Database states that in the year 1951, 1% upper rich people had income equal to the income of bottom 40% people. This scenario has now taken an ominous turn. Now in 2021, 1% upper rich have income equal to the income of the bottom 90% of the people.

Farmers in Punjab, Haryana and western UP grow wheat and paddy because the government provides MSP for these crops, though this MSP is not according to the formula of C2+50% profit on it, but still it obviates the hassles because the government directly purchases them. Hence farmers grow these crops. Paddy crops have depleted the water table in these areas. If the government happens to provide MSP for the remaining 21 other crops as per formula of C2+50% profit on it, then farmers will grow other crops other than wheat and paddy or they will diversify crop growing patterns. The leitmotif is that a mechanism should be arrived at to provide MSP to farmers on all crops with C2+50% profit on it, by granting a legal provision. This will usher in the rise of the income and purchasing power in rural areas to provide fillip to our economy. This will take the country on the path to the much vaunted target of US $ 5 trillion economy.

●●●

42

Analysis of "Repeal and Reform" by Payal Chawla in The Indian Express (18/12/2021)

In her article, Payal Chawla discusses the debate surrounding the repeal of the three farm laws, highlighting the wide variance in estimates regarding the potential cost of Minimum Support Price (MSP) to taxpayers. Estimates range from "trillions of rupees" over the next decade to figures as specific as ₹17 lakh crores and ₹36 thousand crores. This inconsistency underscores a significant disconnect in understanding the impact of MSP among experts and economists.

Historically, India faced severe food shortages, a situation exacerbated by the reliance on monsoon rains for 40% of its food grain production. During times of drought, profiteers and black marketeers would exploit the situation, driving up prices for the common people. It was during Smt. Indira Gandhi's tenure that the government, following advice from the USSR, initiated wholesale procurement of staples like wheat and paddy to stabilize food prices during shortages.

Chawla expresses concern over fears regarding the implementation of MSP for farmers. Currently, the government sets MSP for wheat, paddy, and 21 other crops annually, but only purchases wheat and paddy directly. For the remaining crops, farmers often sell to private traders who do not adhere to the government's MSP, resulting in significantly lower prices that discourage diversification and lead to over-reliance on wheat and paddy. This monoculture has severely depleted the water table in regions like Punjab, Haryana, and western Uttar Pradesh.

The burden on the government for MSP, based on the C2+50% profit formula, would be manageable, given that it primarily purchases wheat and paddy. By legislating this formula, the government would deter traders from exploiting farmers and encourage them to cultivate a wider variety of crops. The current lack of government procurement for the remaining crops places most pricing power in the hands of private traders, leading to unethical price manipulation.

Implementing the C2+50% profit formula would not only protect farmers but also restore public confidence in the government, which is crucial ahead of upcoming assembly elections and the general elections in 2024.

To effectively address the challenges faced by farmers, there is an urgent need for a legal framework that establishes MSP as a minimum price for wheat, paddy, and the 21 other crops, ensuring that no purchases occur below this threshold. With the government responsible primarily for wheat and paddy, the financial implications would be sustainable, shifting the burden to private traders for other crops.

Such legislation would promote economic growth in rural areas, catalyzing demand for finished goods and helping to alleviate the distress that has led to tragic farmer suicides. It would also encourage crop diversification, reducing dependence on imports for items like pulses.

In summary, it is crucial to approach the formulation and implementation of an MSP law with intellectual honesty, aligning with the Swaminathan Commission's recommendations for a C2+50% profit formula. This approach should not be hindered by skepticism from critics who may lack a comprehensive understanding of the agricultural landscape and its challenges.

●●●

43

Through the Lens of Legacy : A Critical Review of The Oxford History of India

I recently acquired *The Oxford History of India* by Vincent A. Smith from Amazon. The interplay between Indian history and geography is profound; as often noted, geography and chronology are the Sun and Moon, the right eye and left eye of all history. India's defining features—its towering Himalayas in the north, the Eastern and Western Ghats, and the Deccan Plateau, along with its snow-fed perennial rivers and fertile deltas—set it apart in the world.

With the exception of China, no region boasts a continuous and unbroken civilization as ancient as that of India. While Egypt and Babylonia may have seen earlier civilized life, the connection between their distant past and the present has long since been severed. In contrast, the ideas from the Vedic period continue to exert a vital influence in contemporary Indian society, and even the rituals of the Rishis persist in practice.

For organizational clarity, Smith divides Indian history into three parts: 1) Ancient and Hindu India, 2) India during the Muslim period, and 3) The British period. In the section on Prehistoric India, he notes that many present-day Rajput castes and clans, including Jats and Gurjars, are descended from the Hun or allied hordes that arrived in ancient times. However, it would enhance future editions to acknowledge the growing perspective that Jats may trace their lineage to either Aryan or Scythian origins. Jats are indeed an ancient people in India, dating back to the time of the Mahabharata War around 3102 BC.

The book references the battle between King Porus and Alexander in 326-327 BC, where Alexander triumphed over Porus, and mentions King Ambhi of Taxila, who made peace with Alexander. However, it omits their identities; contemporary historians increasingly recognize both as Jat rulers. Additionally, while Chandragupta Maurya (321-297 BC), his son Bindusara (297-273 BC), and Emperor Ashoka (268-232 BC) are discussed, their potential identity as Jats is not explored. The same applies to King Kanishka of the Kushan Empire (355-455 AD) and the Gupta dynasty kings—Chandragupta I, Samudragupta, and Chandragupta II—who adopted the title of Vikramaditya. This oversight extends to Yasodharman Virk, a Jat king of Malwa from 528 AD to 543 AD, who notably eliminated the Hun threat from the subcontinent. The book does mention Maharaja Harshvardhana (606-647 AD), identifying him as a Buddhist king from the Bains Jat tribe.

Part II covers the Muslim period, noting Muhammad Ghazni's raids in India (1001-1027 AD). However, it fails to mention that Ghazni's final raid in 1027 AD aimed to punish the Jats of Sindh for their resistance during his campaigns. Ghazni suffered severe injuries during confrontations with the Jats and ultimately died from his wounds in 1030 AD. The book details the first battle of Tarain in 1191 AD, where Muhammad Ghori was defeated by King Prithvi Raj Chauhan, and his subsequent victory over Chauhan in 1192 AD, resulting in the latter's death. Notably absent from this account is the mobilization of Jat resistance under Jatwan Malik, who besieged Hansi Fort and confronted Qutubuddin Aibek in a bloody conflict, ultimately leading to significant casualties from both sides.

The review also mentions the first female Muslim ruler, Razia Begum, without noting that she sought Jat support to reclaim her throne after being deposed. Additionally, while the book highlights Ala-ud-din Khilji's (1296-1316 AD) tax increases from the standard 1/6th to 50%, it neglects to mention the Jat farmers' collective refusal to pay these exorbitant taxes, which led to a significant battle against Khilji's forces, resulting in a decisive Jat victory.

The narrative continues with a discussion on Khokhar tribes, inaccurately omitting their classification as Khokhar Jats. The author states that Ghori was ultimately assassinated by a fanatic while returning from his victorious campaign against the Khokhar Jats. Yet, the historical context reveals that the Khokhar Jats had already defeated Ghori in 1205 AD before he retaliated in 1206 AD. But when Ghori was going victorious to Ghazni he was assassinated by Khokhar Jats.

In discussing Tamerlane's invasion in 1398 AD, the book overlooks the valiant resistance mounted by Khokhar Jats, who faced overwhelming odds but ultimately fell victim to a reportedly brutal genocide. Despite this, the indomitable Jat spirit persisted. This crucial detail should be included in future revisions.

The text mentions the Jat rebellion during Aurangzeb's reign, detailing the uprising led by Gokula in Mathura, which resulted in significant casualties on both sides. It also describes how the Jats plundered Akbar's tomb, signaling profound discontent with Mughal rule.

Smith claims that the Jats abstained from participating in the Third Battle of Panipat in 1761 AD, citing the arrogance of Sada Shiv Rao Bhau as a key factor. However, the book neglects to mention that Maharaja Surajmal refused a substantial payment demanded by Ahmed Shah Abdali, instead asserting that his forts would withstand any attack. Importantly, King Jawahar Singh, Surajmal's son, successfully prevented Abdali from pillaging the holy site of Mathura after a great sanguinary conflict with large casualties from both sides. Additionally, the book fails to acknowledge that Maharaja Surajmal sent Jat escorts to protect Maratha women and children returning to Maharashtra after their defeat, earning the gratitude of the Marathas, who later welcomed the Jats and granted them land and permission to intermarry.

In Part III, which addresses the British period, the narrative frames the British presence as a completed chapter rather than examining the dynamic rise and fall of their rule in India. Crucially, the 1857 uprising is omitted, failing to recognize India's unity amid its diversity. European authors often emphasize diversity over unity, a trend evident in Smith's narrative, which some readers have deemed dull or biased. Nevertheless, others have praised it as a testament to extensive scholarship. While it is a valuable compilation of knowledge, it should acknowledge that India is more than a geographical concept; it is a unified nation with rich diversity.

Overall, while *The Oxford History of India* is a commendable work that displays extensive learning, it would benefit from a more inclusive narrative that recognizes the contributions and significance of various groups, including the Jats, throughout Indian history.

●●●

44

Rediscovering Heritage : A Review of India's Ancient Past by R. S. Sharma

I acquired "India's Ancient Past" by R.S. Sharma from Amazon and have read the entire book without encountering any errors. This work is a remarkable piece of scholarship, praised for its engaging and lucid style. It effectively sheds light on the origins and development of civilizations, empires, and religions in India.

However, I must express my disappointment at the complete absence of the term "JAT" throughout the book. It appears that the Jats have been systematically excluded from the narrative of Indian history, which is disheartening. In reality, theJats are an ancient community with a rich heritage, dating back to the time of the Mahabharata War around 3102 BC. Their omission raises the question: why are they deliberately excluded from historical accounts? The Jats have reportedly historically rejected the notion of Brahmin superiority within the Hindu hierarchy, leading to their exclusion from documented history by Brahmin chroniclers. Historians and enthusiasts should critically examine this omission and seek to address the controversy surrounding it, as it casts a shadow over the credibility of Indian history.

In chapters 18, 19, and 20, King Chandragupta Maurya, King Bindusara, and Emperor Ashoka are discussed. While it is mentioned that Chandragupta Maurya came from a humble background, it should be acknowledged that these rulers were actually of Jat descent. Similarly, King Kanishka of the Kushan dynasty is rightly identified as a Jat. In Chapter 24, which discusses the Gupta Empire (355 AD to 455 AD), the author suggests that the Gupta rulers were of Vaishya origin, which is dubious. Historical evidence supports the view that the Gupta kings were also of Jat origin. Notably, there is no mention of Yasodharman Virk, a Jat ruler of Malwa (now Madhya Pradesh) who effectively eliminated the Hun invaders from India between 528 AD and 543 AD. In Chapter 27, Maharaja Harshvardhana (604 AD to 647 AD) is described as a Buddhist who ruled through a Khap Panchayat. However, labeling him the last great Hindu emperor is misleading; he was neither a devout Hindu nor the ruler of the entire subcontinent.

The book mentions King Porus, who ruled between the Jhelum and Chenab rivers, and Prince Ambhi, the ruler of Taxila. Chapter 16 covers the Iranian and Macedonian invasions, detailing Alexander the Great's campaign against King Porus in 326-327 BC. While the author notes Alexander's initial victory and subsequent restoration of Porus's kingdom, he fails to identify King

Porus and Prince Ambhi as Jats, a critical detail that warrants inclusion.

For organizational clarity, Indian history can be divided into three parts: 1) Ancient History (Buddhist/ Hindu Period), 2) Medieval History (Muslim Period), and 3) Modern Indian History (Arrival of the British). A significant issue within Ancient History is the obfuscation of the identities of rulers as Jats or Gurjars. It is high time to rectify this oversight. The book would greatly benefit from acknowledging and restoring the identities of these kings and emperors as Jats and Gurjars.

●●●

45

Beyond Life and Death : A Review of Death & After by Justice V.R. Krishna Aiyer

During a visit to an exhibition of religious books at Bhartiya Vidya Bhawan on Kasturba Gandhi Marg in New Delhi, I came across a compelling book titled "Death & After" by the Honorable Justice V.R. Krishna Aiyer, a retired Supreme Court judge. Intrigued, I purchased it, and little did I know that this book would profoundly transform my perspective on life and death.

The book includes revelations that extend beyond the scope of Darwinian thought, recounting deeply personal experiences. Justice Aiyer shares the heartbreaking story of his life during the 1970s. His wife, suffering from cancer, was taken to the USA for treatment at the behest of their son, an engineer living there. Despite the efforts made, she ultimately passed away after her condition relapsed.

Upon her death, Justice Aiyer brought her body back to India for cremation. In his grief, he requested a smaller home, resulting in his allocation of a house at 7 Moti Lal Nehru Marg, while his former residence was given to another Supreme Court judge, Justice A.C. Gupta.

The Uncanny Encounter

One night, after a peaceful evening, Justice Gupta and his wife were startled awake by sounds coming from their drawing room. They quickly switched on the lights, only to find a lady in a saree standing before them. To their shock, she introduced herself as Mrs. V.R. Krishna Aiyer, stating that she was already dead and had come to deliver a message to her husband. Just as mysteriously as she appeared, she vanished.

The following morning, Justice Gupta felt compelled to visit Justice Aiyer and relay the extraordinary encounter. Justice Aiyer, initially skeptical but perplexed, pondered the integrity of a respected fellow judge and wondered why he would fabricate such a tale.

Days later, as Justice Gupta and his wife were having dinner, Mrs. Iyer reappeared, cautioning Justice Gupta to warn her husband against driving, as she foresaw an accident. Justice Gupta, filled with urgency, attempted to call Justice Aiyer but was unable to reach him.

Reflections on Life and Beyond

These poignant stories illustrated in Justice Aiyer's book offer a unique lens through which to consider the complexities of death and the possibility of life beyond it. They remind us of the profound connections that endure even after physical separation and challenge our conventional understanding of existence. The book has not only deepened my respect for the mysteries of life but has also instilled a sense of reverence for the memories and legacies of those we love.

●●●

46

Tangled Ties : Understanding India-Pakistan Relations through The People Next Door

In "The People Next Door," former Indian Ambassador T.C.A. Raghavan offers a nuanced exploration of the tumultuous relationship between India and Pakistan over the past seventy years. This comprehensive overview weaves together historical events, cultural intricacies, and personal anecdotes, capturing the essence of a relationship marked by conflict, tragedy, and occasional moments of camaraderie.

Raghavan skillfully discusses critical topics such as the Partition of 1947, the Kashmir conflict, terrorism, and multiple wars, including those in 1948, 1965, and 1971. His writing blends wit with a profound understanding of the complex dynamics at play, presenting a rich tapestry of history that reveals both the absurdities and the tragedies of the bilateral relationship. The author's decision to focus on history rather than policy is evident, as he deliberately concludes the narrative in 2008, suggesting that some aspects of history require time to be fully understood.

The book is organized into eight chapters, beginning with the Partition's harrowing consequences, which led to the displacement of around 12 million people and resulted in widespread violence. Raghavan contrasts this with the relative peace experienced in Malerkotla, a Muslim-majority region that stood as an exception during the chaos. He delves into the accession of Jammu and Kashmir, the lesser-known states of Junagadh and Hyderabad, and the subsequent conflicts that arose.

One of the book's strengths lies in its ability to present historical figures and events with both depth and accessibility. Raghavan touches on the fate of Chaudhary Rahmat Ali, who coined the acronym for Pakistan yet died in obscurity, as well as the controversial life of K.L. Gauba, who converted to Islam but retained his original identity. The narrative captures the complexities of identity and belonging in a fractured subcontinent.

Raghavan does not shy away from the darker chapters of Indo-Pak relations, addressing incidents like the hijacking of Indian Airlines Flight IC-814 and the 26/11 Mumbai attacks, which have left indelible scars on the relationship. His recounting of lighter, yet telling, anecdotes—such as the dacoit Bhupet Daku's escapades—provides a counterpoint to the more serious discussions, illustrating the often absurd nature of geopolitical tensions.

Through clever storytelling, Raghavan emphasizes the entrenched nature of the Kashmir issue, highlighted by General Zia Ul Haq's infamous assertion that "Kashmir is in my blood." This metaphorical dialogue between Zia and Indian High Commissioner K. Natwar Singh encapsulates the ongoing struggle for resolution and peace.

While Raghavan poses the critical question of whether lasting peace is achievable between these two neighbors, he refrains from providing definitive answers. Instead, he leaves readers to reflect on the complexities of the situation. The book serves as a vital resource for anyone interested in understanding the intricate web of historical and contemporary factors that shape India-Pakistan relations.

Overall, "The People Next Door" is a remarkable achievement in scholarship, balancing historical rigor with engaging prose. It is an essential read for diplomats, historians, and anyone keen to comprehend the nuances of one of the world's most challenging geopolitical landscapes.

●●●

47

Navigating Change : Key Lessons from Global Turning Points by Mauro Guillen and Emilio Ontiveros

In "Global Turning Points," Mauro Guillen and Emilio Ontiveros provide a thought-provoking exploration of significant shifts that have reshaped human societies. Though published in 2016, the book presciently anticipates the profound changes that have occurred since then, particularly emphasizing that the COVID-19 pandemic will likely emerge as a seminal inflection point, even more significant than events like the assassination of Archduke Ferdinand in 1914 or the rise of Adolf Hitler in 1933.

The authors outline several critical turning points that have transformed global dynamics, including the 9/11 terrorist attacks and China's entry into the World Trade Organization shortly thereafter. They highlight a range of social, economic, and environmental trends that are redefining the 21st century:

Urbanization: For the first time, more people live in cities than in rural areas, indicating a shift in lifestyle and societal structure.

Obesity vs. Hunger: A striking observation is that more individuals globally suffer from obesity than from hunger, reflecting changing health crises.

Emerging Economies: The authors note that emerging economies now account for half of the global economy, with projections that India will soon become the most populous country and China the largest in output.

Inequality and Environmental Challenges: They discuss deepening inequalities within countries and the impending challenges of food and water shortages, emphasizing the urgency for corrective action to combat climate change.

The book delves into the implications of these trends, examining phenomena such as population aging, government gridlock, and the breakdown of state authority. The authors argue that since World War II, more countries have experienced state failure than have been governed by dictators, underscoring a complex global landscape.

Guillen and Ontiveros also explore the rise of a global middle class across regions like Brazil, Mexico, China, and India, predicting that by 2027, over half the world's population will belong to this demographic. Additionally, they address the digital divide, illustrating stark contrasts between mobile broadband access in developed and developing nations.

Overall, "Global Turning Points" is an engaging and erudite examination of the multifaceted challenges facing humanity in the 21st century. The authors' ability to weave together diverse themes—society, business, politics, and environment—makes for a compelling narrative. Their call for awareness and action regarding these turning points is both urgent and necessary.

This book is a must-read for anyone seeking to understand the complexities of our current era and the pivotal moments that have shaped, and will continue to shape, our world.

48

Wealth and Inequality : A Deep Dive into The Billionaire Raj by James Crabtree

James Crabtree's "The Billionaire Raj" offers a compelling exploration of the rise of India's super-rich amid a backdrop of stark inequality. The book vividly illustrates the transformation of India into a nation where immense wealth coexists with widespread poverty, embodied by the likes of Mukesh Ambani's opulent residence, Antilia, a potent symbol of this new era.

Crabtree traces the roots of this disparity, highlighting the shift that began in the early 2000s, when a globally connected elite began to flourish. He juxtaposes India's current wealth concentration with its past—an era where the nation was relatively egalitarian in the immediate post-Independence period. The author's use of phrases like "island of California in a sea of sub-Saharan Africa" poignantly captures the paradox of modern India, where a burgeoning wealthy class thrives amidst overwhelming poverty.

The statistics presented are staggering: the top one percent of earners now control over half of the national wealth, echoing concerns raised by economists about the country's rising inequality. Crabtree notes that India, alongside South Africa and Brazil, ranks among the world's least equal nations. This grim reality raises questions about social stability and economic progress, especially in light of recent research suggesting that inequality stifles growth and creates divisions that hinder reform.

Central to Crabtree's analysis is the phenomenon of crony capitalism—where political and business elites collude to amass wealth at the expense of the public. He details the systemic corruption that has flourished alongside economic liberalization, with myriad scandals highlighting how tycoons have leveraged their connections to gain access to resources and contracts. The author paints a picture of a nation where retail corruption has evolved into wholesale graft, touching every sector from mining to public services.

Drawing parallels with America's Gilded Age, Crabtree suggests that India is at a similar crossroads. The comparison is apt; just as the late 19th-century U.S. grappled with its own elite and political corruption, so too does India face the challenge of addressing its burgeoning inequality. The future of India's democracy hinges on whether it can escape this cycle of corruption and inequity.

As the book progresses, Crabtree raises critical questions about India's trajectory. Will the nation emerge from this Gilded Age into a Progressive Era, addressing the perils of inequality and crony capitalism? Or will it remain mired in the excesses of the past, potentially leading to a socio-political landscape reminiscent of authoritarian regimes?

In conclusion, "The Billionaire Raj" is an insightful, well-researched examination of India's socio-economic landscape. Crabtree's engaging narrative weaves together statistics, anecdotes, and historical context to paint a vivid picture of a country at a pivotal moment in its history. This book is essential reading for anyone seeking to understand the complexities of modern India, its wealthy elite, and the broader implications for its future as a global power.

●●●

49

Historical Gaps in NCERT's "Our Pasts": The Untold Stories of Jat Resistance and Leadership

The NCERT history textbooks, Our Pasts I, Our Pasts II, and Our Pasts III, prescribed for classes VI to VIII, provide an essential overview of India's ancient, medieval, and modern history. However, upon reviewing these books, it becomes clear that several key figures and events, particularly concerning the Jat community, have been overlooked. These omissions result in an incomplete portrayal of India's history, especially regarding the contributions of local heroes and regional resistance movements.

Our Pasts I : Ancient India

Our Pasts I begins by introducing the nomenclature of India, derived from the Indus River, and proceeds to explore the early history of the subcontinent, including the Harappan civilization and the Vedic period. However, it fails to connect several significant figures and events to their proper historical context. For instance, the book overlooks the possible connection between the Mauryan rulers, such as Chandragupta Maurya and Ashoka, and the Jat tribes. Similarly, it misses critical details about King Kanishka and Yasodharman Virk, both significant rulers with ties to the Jat community.

The book also provides minimal coverage of the South Indian dynasties, such as the Pallavas and Chalukyas, while ignoring important figures like King Harshavardhana, a Buddhist Jat king. Furthermore, the omission of Jat King Sahasi Ray of Sindh, and his struggles against treachery from the Brahmin priest Rai Chach, leaves out an important chapter in early medieval Indian history. These gaps prevent students from gaining a comprehensive understanding of the early history of India, especially in terms of regional governance and resistance movements.

Our Pasts II : Medieval India

Our Pasts II covers the medieval period and the arrival of Muslim rulers in India, yet it fails to adequately highlight the Jat community's role in resisting foreign invaders. For example, Mahmud Ghazni's invasions (1001–1027 AD) are briefly mentioned, but the book omits his last campaign against the Jats of Sindh, which resulted in significant resistance. The Jat-led rebellion against Ghazni's forces is a crucial event that illustrates the strength of regional opposition to foreign conquest, yet it is not included.

The book also misses the Jat resistance against Tamarlane in 1398 AD, and the rebellion led by Jatwan Malik after the defeat of Prithviraj Chauhan at the Second Battle of Tarain in 1192 AD. Furthermore, it glosses over the Khokhar Jats' victory over Muhammad Ghori in 1205 AD and their assassination of him in 1206 AD. These events were pivotal in shaping the medieval political landscape, yet they remain underrepresented.

Additionally, the book fails to mention the rebellion of the Jats under Gokula in 1660 AD, which forced the Mughal Emperor Aurangzeb to shift his capital from Delhi to Agra. The absence of Maharaja Surajmal's significant role in resisting Mughal forces during the Maratha invasion in the Third Battle of Panipat (1761) is another major omission. Surajmal's warfare strategies and his contributions to the Jat cause are pivotal yet ignored in the curriculum.

Our Pasts III : Modern India

Our Pasts III focuses on the British colonial period and the struggle for independence. While the book provides a broad overview of key events like the Revolt of 1857 and it fails to mention the contributions of several Jat leaders and others who played pivotal roles in the Revolt of 1857 notably figures such as Raja Nahar Singh of Faridabad, Raja Bahadur Singh Thakran of Gurgaon, Raja Amani Singh of Aligarh, Raja Mohan Singh of Shamli, Raja Dev

Singh of Mathura, Raja Dev Karan Singh of Sadabad, Chaudhary Ram Singh Maan of Balla village Karnal, Jat sisters Shiv Devi age 16 years and Jai Devi age 14 years, Chaudhary Udmi Ram of Livaspur village near Sonipat and Rao Tula Ram of Rewari who led the resistance in Haryana and surrounding areas, are absent from the narrative. These leaders' efforts were crucial in the 1857 uprising and its aftermath, and their omission reflects a significant gap in the history being taught.

The book also overlooks the Battle of Saragarhi (1897), where 21 Jat Sikh soldiers heroically defended against a much larger Afghan force. Similarly, the sacrifices made by Indian soldiers during World War I and II, especially by Jat soldiers, are not mentioned. Around 87,000 Indians perished in World War I and 74,187 in World War II, with a significant portion of these soldiers being Jats. These contributions to global peace deserve recognition but remain largely unacknowledged in the textbook.

Additionally, the book neglects the roles of figures like Maharaja Ranjit Singh, Maharaja Mahendra Pratap, and Sir Chhotu Ram, who made lasting contributions to India's freedom struggle and agricultural reforms. Maharaja Ranjit Singh's military prowess is compared to Napoleon's, yet his contributions are not fully appreciated in the curriculum. The absence of Sir Chhotu Ram's efforts to unite farmers and create landmark legislation in Punjab is another oversight that detracts from the completeness of the narrative.

Conclusion : A Need for a More Inclusive History

In conclusion, while the NCERT textbooks Our Pasts I, Our Pasts II, and Our Pasts III offer a broad and essential framework for understanding India's past, they fall short in certain areas, particularly regarding the contributions of the Jat community. The omissions of pivotal figures and events—ranging from ancient Indian rulers to leaders in the fight against colonial rule—undermine the accuracy and completeness of the historical narrative. These gaps hinder students from forming a fuller understanding of the past, especially the regional resistance movements and the complex interplay of different communities in shaping India's history.

A more inclusive approach is necessary, one that acknowledges the contributions of all communities, including the Jats, in India's long and varied history. Such an approach would offer students a richer, more nuanced view of the past, fostering a deeper appreciation for the diverse forces that shaped the nation.

50

References

While a lot what I have written stems from memory and the sheer number of books I have read in my lifetime, I would like to specifically acknowledge the following sources that have been consulted during the course of writing this book:

1. History of the Jats by K.R.Qanungo
2. Maharaja Surajmal by K. Natwar Singh
3. Later Mughals by William Irwine
4. Deeg by M.C. Joshi
5. History of Aurangzeb (5 volumes) Jadunath Sarkar
6. Annals and Antiquities of Rajasthan by Colonel James Tod
7. An account of the Jat kingdom by Father Xavier Wendel
8. Mathura- A District Memoir by F.S. Growse
9. The Jats- their role in the Mughal Empire by Girish Chandra Dwivedi

10. Bharatpur upto 1826: a social and political history of Jats by Ram Pande
11. Archaeological survey of India report (1882-86) volume XX by Alexander Cunningham
12. Bharatpur- a saga of invincible courage by C.S. Verma
13. Oxford history of India by Vincent A. Smith
14. History of Sikhs vol 1 & 11 by Khushwant Singh
15. Ethnology of Jats by Chaudhuri Lahri Singh.
16. Untold Story by Lt. General B.M. Kaul
17. Himalayan Blunder by Brigadier J.P. Dalvi
18. India- China War by Neville Maxwell.
19. Jats- the ancient rulers (a clan study) by Bhim Singh Dahiya.
20. Fall of the Mughal Empire (4 volumes) by Jadunath Sarkar

●●●